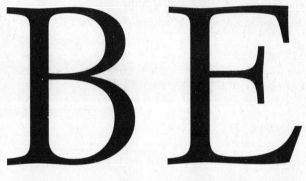

BE
DILIGENT

SERVING OTHERS AS YOU WALK WITH THE
MASTER SERVANT

NT COMMENTARY

MARK

Warren W. Wiersbe

David C Cook®
transforming lives together

BE DILIGENT
Published by David C Cook
4050 Lee Vance View
Colorado Springs, CO 80918 U.S.A.

David C Cook Distribution Canada
55 Woodslee Avenue, Paris, Ontario, Canada N3L 3E5

David C Cook U.K., Kingsway Communications
Eastbourne, East Sussex BN23 6NT, England

The graphic circle C logo is a registered trademark of David C Cook.

Unless otherwise noted, all Scripture quotations are taken from the King James Version of the
Bible. (Public Domain.) Scripture quotations marked NASB are taken from the *New American
Standard Bible*, © Copyright 1960, 1995 by The Lockman Foundation. Used by permission;
and NIV are taken from the *Holy Bible, New International Version*®. *NIV*®. Copyright ©
1973, 1978, 1984 International Bible Society. Used by permission of Zondervan. All
rights reserved. The author has added italics to Scripture quotations for emphasis.

LCCN 2009934567
ISBN 978-1-4347-6631-1
eISBN 978-1-4347-0091-9

First edition of *Be Diligent* by Warren W. Wiersbe published by Victor Books®
in 1987 © Warren W. Wiersbe, ISBN 0-89693-356-3

The Team: Karen Lee-Thorp, Amy Kiechlin, Sarah Schultz, Jack Campbell, and Karen Athen
Series Cover Design: John Hamilton Design
Cover Photo: Veer Inc.

Printed in the United States of America
Second Edition 2010

6 7 8 9 10 11 12

040814

BE
DILIGENT

To

Gale and Millie Baldridge

*longtime friends from seminary days whose ministry
exemplifies true servanthood (Hebrews 6:10)*

CONTENTS

THE BIG IDEA

An Introduction to *Be Diligent*
by Ken Baugh

The Princess Bride is one of my favorite movies because it exemplifies true love. As the story begins, young Wesley is the servant of a beautiful girl named Buttercup. Of course, Wesley is madly in love with Buttercup and is eager to please her in every way. When she asks him to do mundane tasks with a demanding and condescending tone in her voice he simply responds, "as you wish." As the story continues, Wesley wins Buttercup's heart with his servant attitude and gentle spirit. I know, that's mush, but there's a lot of action in the movie too: a voyage through the sea of insanity, a death-defying journey through the fire swamp, sword fights between good guys and bad guys, betrayal, kidnapping, torture, even Rodents of Unusual Size. This movie's got it all, all the things that make up a good fairy tale. But what I like most about it (in addition to all the action) is the fact that the boy wins the girl's heart through loving acts of service.

As a senior pastor, I have often wondered about the best way to win the hearts of people to Christ. Is it through great worship services, solid Bible teaching, relevant programs, or the bold proclamation of the gospel? Of course, all these elements play a role in winning people's hearts to Christ, but I can't help but wonder if we're missing something, because there are lots of churches that provide all these things, yet statistically, church attendance in America is declining, and more and more people are turning to alternate forms of spirituality rather than the person and work of Jesus Christ.

Could it be, at least in part, that people are turning away from Jesus and His church because we as His followers have neglected to develop the one character trait that Jesus modeled for us over and over again? Could it be that the reason people flocked to Jesus was because He personified this all-important character trait? Could it be that this particular trait is the one that really gets people's attention, because when it is lived out, it is so countercultural that people can't help but notice and attribute its presence to something supernatural?

What is this character trait? Servanthood. I believe that servanthood is the character trait that wins the hearts of people who are looking for a faith that is real. And John Mark, the guy who wrote the gospel of Mark, believed that too. Let me explain.

Throughout Mark's gospel, we discover the true character of Jesus Christ as a servant. Where Matthew wrote to a Jewish audience and painted Christ as the long-awaited Messiah who came through David's line and fulfilled the promises of the Old Testament prophets, Mark wrote to a Roman audience who had little interest in a Jewish Messiah but a lot of interest in the story of this servant named Jesus. There is no genealogy in Mark's gospel because a servant's lineage is of little consequence. There is no mention of Jesus' birth when kings came to worship Him and brought gifts of gold, frankincense, and myrrh, because kings from afar don't pay homage to servants. In Mark's gospel, there is no mention of Jesus' noble rights as the King of Kings.

Instead, Mark's focus is on the character of this man named Jesus. Mark affirms that Jesus is most certainly the Messiah (Mark 8:29), God's Son (Mark 1:10–11), the one and only God-man, fully human and fully divine, performing miracles that only God could perform. To emphasize Jesus' deity, Mark records that Jesus cast out demons (1:21–28), healed the sick (1:32–34), made the lepers clean (1:40–45), made a paralyzed man walk (2:1–12), calmed a storm at sea (4:35–41), brought a young girl back from the dead (5:35–43), fed five thousand people with a small amount of food (6:32–44), and walked on water (6:45–51). But instead of painting a portrait of the Christ as the King, Mark paints a portrait of the Christ as a suffering servant (Mark 8:31) who came to win the hearts and ransom the lives of people through His loving act of service as He gave His life on the cross to pay the price for their sin. In fact, Mark records Jesus' own summation of His earthly purpose: "For even the Son of Man did not come to be served, but to serve, and to give his life as a ransom for many" (Mark 10:45 NIV). Here we see three characteristics of servanthood that Jesus modeled for us and will live out through us as we devote ourselves to His service.

The three characteristics of a servant that draw people to Jesus:

1. A willingness to help others first. Jesus as a servant said, "For even the Son of Man did not come to be served" (Mark 10:45 NIV). To be selfless is to look to meet the needs of others before meeting your own. As you read through Mark's gospel, watch for evidence of Jesus' selfless lifestyle, and identify ways that you can serve others in the same way.

2. A willingness to meet others' practical needs. Jesus as a servant came "to serve," and He did so by being aware of the practical, everyday needs of the people around Him: their need for food, for comfort, for encouragement and guidance. As God in human flesh, Jesus was able to meet people's practical needs in miraculous ways that we cannot, but there certainly are things that we can be aware of and respond to. As you read through Mark's gospel, look for practical ways that Jesus met people's everyday needs, and then identify ways that you can serve others in a similar manner.

3. A willingness to give sacrificially to others. Jesus as a servant came

to give His life for others. We know that Jesus sacrificed His life as a sin offering for all who would believe in Him; it was the greatest sacrificial act of service in the history of humanity. Maybe the greatest sacrificial act that we can bestow on another person is to take the chance to share the gospel with them. To risk their rejection, their ridicule, even abuse, because we are willing to sacrifice ourselves for their eternal destiny.

Jesus was the suffering Servant, and He modeled for us the most important way to win people's hearts for Him: through loving acts of service. I pray that as you study Mark's gospel, you will look for ways to emulate the greatest Servant who ever lived, our Lord and Savior Jesus Christ.

***

Dr. Wiersbe's commentaries have been a source of guidance and strength to me over the many years that I have been a pastor. His unique style is not overly academic, but theologically sound. He explains the deep truths of Scripture in a way that everyone can understand and apply. Whether you're a Bible scholar or a brand-new believer in Christ, you will benefit, as I have, from Warren's insights. With your Bible in one hand and Dr. Wiersbe's commentary in the other, you will be able to accurately unpack the deep truths of God's Word and learn how to apply them to your life.

Drink deeply, my friend, of the truths of God's Word, for in them you will find Jesus Christ, and there is freedom, peace, assurance, and joy.

—Ken Baugh
Pastor of Coast Hills Community Church
Aliso Viejo, California

A WORD FROM THE AUTHOR

The gospel of Mark is just the book for busy people who want to use every opportunity to serve God. It presents our Lord "on the move," meeting the physical and spiritual needs of all kinds of people. Mark depicts Him as God's suffering Servant who came, not to be ministered to, but to minister—even to the extent of giving His life for us on the cross.

Our world is filled with hurting people who need our ministry. Jesus left His church on earth so that we might continue the ministry He started. However, I fear that in the church today, we have too many spectators and not enough participants, too many celebrities and not enough servants.

This was the first of my "BE" books to be written on a word processor, and this would have been very difficult for me were it not for the able assistance of my neighbor, Scott Florell, who is a computer expert. At the time, Scott was a busy student at the University of Nebraska, but he took time to teach me and help me understand and solve my computer problems. This is but one of many ways in which Scott has enriched our lives, and I want to register my appreciation here.

If our time together studying Mark's gospel in this volume encourages you to be diligent in your own ministry to others, then the time has not been wasted. May our Lord enable all of us to be servants for His glory!

—Warren W. Wiersbe

A Suggested Outline of the Book of Mark

Theme: Jesus Christ the Servant
Key verse: Mark 10:45

I.   The Presentation of the Servant (Mark 1:1–13)
II. The Servant's Ministry in Galilee (Mark 1:14—9:50)
    1.   Period of popularity (Mark 1:14—6:29)
    2.   Period of withdrawal (Mark 6:30—9:32)
    3.   Period of completion (Mark 9:33–50)
III. The Servant's Journey to Jerusalem (Mark 10)
IV. The Servant's Ministry in Jerusalem (Mark 11—16)
    1.   Public teaching and controversy (Mark 11:1—12:44)
    2.   Private teaching and ministry (Mark 13:1—14:31)
    3.   Arrest, trial, and crucifixion (Mark 14:32—15:47)
    4.   Resurrection and ascension (Mark 16)

Chapter One

GOD'S SERVANT IS HERE!

(Mark 1)

T he gospel is neither a discussion nor a debate," said Dr. Paul S. Rees. "It is an announcement!"

Mark wasted no time giving that announcement, for it is found in the opening words of his book. Matthew, who wrote primarily for the Jews, opened his book with a genealogy. After all, he had to prove to his readers that Jesus Christ is indeed the rightful Heir to David's throne.

Since Luke focused mainly on the sympathetic ministry of the Son of Man, he devoted the early chapters of his book to a record of the Savior's birth. Luke emphasized Christ's humanity, for he knew that his Greek readers would identify with the perfect Babe who grew up to be the perfect Man.

John's gospel begins with a statement about eternity. Why? Because John wrote to prove to the whole world that Jesus Christ of Nazareth is the Son of God (John 20:31). The *subject* of John's gospel is the deity of Christ, but the *object* of his gospel is to encourage his readers to believe on this Savior and receive the gift of eternal life.

Where does Mark's gospel fit in? Mark wrote for the Romans, and his theme is *Jesus Christ the Servant*. If we had to pick a "key verse" in this gospel, it would be Mark 10:45—"For even the Son of man came not to be ministered unto, but to minister, and to give his life a ransom for many."

The fact that Mark wrote with the Romans in mind helps us understand his style and approach. The emphasis in this gospel is on *activity*. Mark describes Jesus as He busily moves from place to place and meets the physical and spiritual needs of all kinds of people. One of Mark's favorite words is "straightway," meaning "immediately." He uses it forty-one times. Mark does not record many of our Lord's sermons because his emphasis is on what Jesus did rather than what Jesus said. He reveals Jesus as God's Servant, sent to minister to suffering people and to die for the sins of the world. Mark gives us no account of our Lord's birth, nor does he record a genealogy, unnecessary in regard to a servant.

In this opening chapter, Mark shares three important facts about God's Servant.

1. THE SERVANT'S IDENTITY (1:1–11)

How does Mark identify this Servant? He records the testimonies of several dependable witnesses to assure us that Jesus is all that He claims to be.

John Mark, the author of the book, is the first witness (v. 1). He states boldly that Jesus Christ is the Son of God. It is likely that Mark was an eyewitness of some of the events that he wrote about. He lived in Jerusalem with his mother, Mary, and their home was a meeting place for believers in the city (Acts 12:1–19). Several scholars believe that Mark was the young man described in Mark 14:51–52. Since Peter called Mark "my son" (1 Peter 5:13), it is probable that it was Peter who led Mark to faith in Jesus Christ. Church tradition states that Mark was "Peter's interpreter," so that the gospel of Mark reflects the personal experiences and witness of Simon Peter.

The word *gospel* simply means "the good news." To the Romans, Mark's special target audience, *gospel* meant "joyful news about the emperor." The "gospel of Jesus Christ" is the good news that God's Son has come into the world and died for our sins. It is the good news that our sins can be forgiven, that we can belong to the family of God and one day go to live with God in heaven. It is the announcement of victory over sin, death, and hell (1 Cor. 15:1–8, 51–52; Gal. 1:1–9).

The second witness is that of the prophets (vv. 2–3). Mark cites two quotations from the Old Testament prophets, Malachi 3:1 and Isaiah 40:3 (note also Ex. 23:20). The words *messenger* and *voice* refer to John the Baptist, the prophet God sent to prepare the way for His Son (Matt. 3; Luke 3:1–18; John 1:19–34). In ancient times, before a king visited any part of his realm, a messenger was sent before him to prepare the way. This included both repairing the roads and preparing the people. By calling the nation to repentance, John the Baptist prepared the way for the Lord Jesus Christ. Isaiah and Malachi join voices in declaring that Jesus Christ is the Lord, Jehovah God.

John the Baptist is the next witness (vv. 4–8). Jesus called him the greatest of the prophets (Matt. 11:1–15). In his dress, manner of life, and message of repentance, John identified with Elijah (2 Kings 1:8; Mal. 4:5; Matt. 17:10–13; and note Luke 1:13–17). The "wilderness" where John ministered is the rugged wasteland along the western shore of the Dead Sea. John was telling the people symbolically that they were in a "spiritual wilderness" far worse than the physical wilderness that their ancestors had endured for forty years. John called the people to leave their spiritual wilderness, trust their "Joshua" (Jesus), and enter into their inheritance.

John was careful to magnify Jesus and not himself (see John 3:25–30). John would baptize repentant sinners in water, but "the coming One" would baptize them with the Spirit (Acts 1:4–5). This did not mean that John's baptism was unauthorized (see Matt. 21:23–27), or that water baptism would one day be replaced by Spirit baptism (see Matt. 28:19–20). Rather, John's message and baptism were *preparation* so that the people would be ready to meet and trust the Messiah, Jesus Christ. Our Lord's apostles were no doubt baptized by John (see John 4:1–2; Acts 1:21–26).

The Father and the Holy Spirit are Mark's final witnesses to the identity of God's Servant (vv. 9–11). When Jesus was baptized, the Spirit came on Him as a dove, and the Father spoke from heaven and identified His beloved Son. The people who were there did not hear the voice or see the dove, but Jesus and John did (see John 1:29–34). The word *beloved* not only declares affection, but it also carries the meaning of "the only one." The Father's announcement from heaven reminds us of Psalm 2:7 and Isaiah 42:1.

You will want to note these references in Mark's gospel to Jesus Christ as the Son of God: Mark 1:1, 11; 3:11; 5:7; 9:7; 12:1–11; 13:32; 14:61–62; and 15:39. Mark did not write his book about just any Jewish servant. He wrote his book about the very Son of God who came from heaven to die for the sins of the world.

Yes, Jesus is the Servant—but He is a most unusual Servant. After all, it is the servant who prepares the way for others and announces their arrival. But *others* prepared the way for Jesus and announced that He had come! Even heaven itself took note of Him! This Servant is God the Son.

2. The Servant's Authority (1:12–28)

We expect a servant to be *under* authority and to *take* orders, but God's Servant *exercises* authority and *gives* orders—even to demons—and His orders are obeyed. In this section, Mark describes three scenes that reveal our Lord's authority as the Servant of God.

(1) His temptation (vv. 12–13). Mark does not give as full an account of the temptation as do Matthew (4:1–11) and Luke (4:1–13), but Mark adds some vivid details that the others omit. The Spirit "driveth him" into the wilderness. Mark used this strong word eleven times to describe the casting out of demons. The New American Standard Version has it *impelled,* and the New International Version translates it *sent*. It does not suggest that our Lord was either unwilling or afraid to face Satan. Rather, it is Mark's way of showing the intensity of the experience. No time was spent basking in the glory of the heavenly voice or the presence of the heavenly dove. The Servant had a task to perform and He immediately went to do it.

In concise form, Mark presents us with two symbolic pictures. Our Lord's forty *days* in the wilderness remind us of Israel's forty *years* in the wilderness. Israel failed when they were tested, but our Lord succeeded victoriously. Having triumphed over the enemy, Jesus could now go forth and call a new people who would enter into their spiritual inheritance. Since the name *Jesus* is the Greek form of "Joshua," we can see the parallel.

The second picture is that of the "last Adam" (1 Cor. 15:45). The first Adam was tested in a beautiful Garden and failed, but Jesus was tempted in a dangerous wilderness and won the victory. Adam lost his "dominion" over creation because of his sin (Gen. 1:28; Ps. 8), but in Christ, that dominion has been restored for all who trust Him (Heb. 2:6–8). Jesus was with the wild beasts and they did not harm Him. He gave a demonstration of that future time of peace and righteousness, when the Lord shall return and establish His kingdom (Isa. 11:9; 35:9). Indeed, He is a Servant with authority!

(2) His preaching (vv. 14–22). If ever a man spoke God's truth with authority, it was Jesus Christ (see Matt. 7:28–29). It has been said that the scribes spoke *from* authorities but that Jesus spoke *with* authority. Mark was not recording here the beginning of our Lord's ministry, since He had already ministered in other places (John 1:35—4:4). He is telling us why Jesus left Judea and came to Galilee: Herod had arrested John the Baptist, and wisdom dictated that Jesus relocate. By the way, it was during this journey that Jesus talked with the Samaritan woman (John 4:1–45).

Our Lord's message was the gospel of the kingdom of God, or "the gospel of God" as some texts read. No doubt most of the Jews read "political revolution" into the phrase "kingdom of God," but that was not what Jesus had in mind at all. His kingdom has to do with His reign in the lives of His people; it is a spiritual realm and not a political organization. The only way to enter God's kingdom is by believing the good news and being born again (John 3:1–7).

The gospel is called "the gospel of God" because it comes from God and brings us to God. It is "the gospel of the kingdom" because faith in the Savior brings you into His kingdom. It is the "gospel of Jesus Christ" because He is the heart of it; without His life, death, and resurrection, there would be no good news. Paul called it "the gospel of the grace of God" (Acts 20:24) because there can be no salvation apart from grace (Eph. 2:8–9). There is only one gospel (Gal. 1:1–9), and it centers in what Jesus Christ did for us on the cross (1 Cor. 15:1–11).

Jesus preached that people should repent (change their minds) and believe (see Acts 20:21). Repentance alone is not enough to save us, even though God expects believers to turn from their sins. We must also put positive faith in Jesus Christ and believe His promise of salvation. Repentance without faith could become remorse, and remorse can destroy people who carry a burden of guilt (see Matt. 27:3–5; 2 Cor. 7:8–10).

Because Jesus preached with authority, He was able to call men from their regular occupations and make them His disciples. Who else could interrupt four fishermen at their work and challenge them to leave their nets and follow Him? Several months before, Jesus had already met Peter, Andrew, James, and John, and they had come to trust Him (see John 1:35–49). This was not their initial call to faith and salvation; it was an initial call to discipleship. The fact that Zebedee had hired servants suggests that his fishing business was successful and that he was a man of means. It also assures us that James and John did not mistreat their father when they heeded Christ's call. With the help of his servants, Zebedee could still manage the business.

Jesus did not invent the term "fishers of men." In that day, it was a common description of philosophers and other teachers who "captured men's minds" through teaching and persuasion. They would "bait the hook" with their teachings and "catch" disciples. It is likely that as many as seven of our Lord's disciples were fishermen (John 21:1–3). Surely the good qualities of successful fishermen would make for success in the difficult ministry of winning lost souls: courage, the ability to work together, patience, energy, stamina, faith, and tenacity. Professional fishermen simply could not afford to be quitters or complainers!

Jesus ministered not only in the open air but also in the synagogues. The Jewish synagogues developed during the nation's exile when the people were in Babylon after the temple had been destroyed. Wherever there were ten Jewish men above the age of twelve, a synagogue could be organized. The synagogue was not a place of sacrifice—that was done at the temple—but of reading the Scriptures, praying, and worshipping God. The services were led, not by priests, but by laymen, and the ministry was supervised by a board of elders that was presided over by a "ruler" (Mark 5:22). It was customary to ask visiting rabbis to read the Scriptures and teach, which explains why Jesus had such freedom to minister in the synagogues. The apostle Paul also took advantage of this privilege (Acts 13:14–16; 14:1; 17:1–4).

Our Lord had set up His headquarters in Capernaum, possibly in or near the home of Peter and Andrew (Mark 1:29). You may see the remains of a Capernaum synagogue when you visit the Holy Land today, but it is not the one in which Jesus worshipped. The people assembled for services on the Sabbath as well as on Mondays and Thursdays. Being a faithful Jew, Jesus honored the Sabbath by going to the synagogue, and when He taught the Word, the people were astonished at His authority.

You will discover as you read Mark's gospel that he delights in recording the emotional responses of people. The congregation in the synagogue was "astonished" at His teaching and "amazed" at His healing powers (Mark 1:27; also note 2:12; 5:20, 42; 6:2, 51; 7:37; 10:26; 11:18). You even find Mark recording our Lord's amazement at the unbelief of the people in Nazareth (Mark 6:6). There is certainly nothing monotonous about this narrative!

(3) His command (vv. 23–28). We wonder how many synagogue services that man had attended without revealing that he was demonized. It took the presence of the Son of God to expose the demon, and Jesus not only exposed him, but He also commanded him to keep quiet about His identity and to depart from the man. The Savior did not want, nor did He need, the assistance of Satan and his army to tell people who He was (see Acts 16:16–24).

The demon certainly knew exactly who Jesus was (see Acts 19:13–17) and that he had nothing in common with Him. The demon's use of plural pronouns shows how closely he was identified with the man through whom he was speaking. The demon clearly identified Christ's humanity ("Jesus of Nazareth") as well as His deity ("the Holy One of God"). He also confessed great fear that Jesus might judge him and send him to the pit. There are people today just like this demonized man: in a religious meeting, able to tell who Jesus is, and even trembling with fear of judgment—yet lost (see James 2:19).

"Hold thy peace!" literally means "Be muzzled!" Jesus would use the same words when stilling the storm (Mark 4:39). The demon tried one last convulsive attack, but then had to submit to the authority of God's Servant and come out of the man. The people in the synagogue were amazed and afraid. They realized that something new had appeared on the scene—a new doctrine and a new power. Our Lord's *words and works* must always go together (John 3:2). The people kept on talking about both, and the fame of Jesus began to spread. Our Lord did not encourage this kind of public excitement lest it create problems with both the Jews and the Romans. The

Jews would want to follow Him only because of His power to heal them, and the Romans would think He was a Jewish insurrectionist trying to overthrow the government. This explains why Jesus so often told people to keep quiet (Mark 1:44; 3:12; 5:43; 7:36–37; 8:26, 30; 9:9). The fact that they did not obey created problems for Him.

3. THE SERVANT'S SYMPATHY (1:29–45)

Two miracles of healing are described in this section, both of which reveal the compassion of the Savior for those in need. In fact, so great was His love for the needy that the Savior ministered to great crowds of people after the Sabbath had ended, when it was lawful for them to come for help. It would appear that God's Servant was at the beck and call of all kinds of people, including demoniacs and lepers, and He lovingly ministered to them all.

Jesus and the four disciples left the synagogue and went to Peter and Andrew's house for their Sabbath meal. Perhaps Peter was a bit apologetic because his wife had to care for her sick mother and was unable to entertain them in the usual manner. We do not know about the other disciples, but we do know that Peter was a married man (Mark 1:30).

Peter and Andrew not only brought their friends James and John home with them from the service, but they also brought the Lord home. That is a good example for us to follow: Don't leave Jesus at the church—take Him home with you and let Him share your blessings and your burdens. What a privilege it was for Peter and his family to have the very Son of God as a guest in their humble home. Before long, the Guest became the Host, just as one day the Passenger in Peter's boat would become the Captain (Luke 5:1–11).

By faith, the men told Jesus about the sick woman, no doubt expecting Him to heal her. That is exactly what He did! The fever left her immediately, and she was able to go to the kitchen and serve the Sabbath meal. If you have ever had a bad fever, then you know how painful and uncomfortable it is. You also know that after the fever leaves you, it takes time for you to regain your strength. But not so in this case! She was able to serve the Lord immediately. And isn't service to our Lord one of the best ways to thank Him for all He has done for us?

What was the result of this miracle? When the Sabbath ended at sundown, the whole city showed up at Peter's door! They brought their sick and afflicted, and the Lord (who was no doubt weary) healed them all. The Greek verb indicates that they "kept on bringing" people to Him, so that He must have gone to sleep at a very late hour. Note in Mark 1:32 the clear distinction made between the diseased and the demonized. While Satan can cause physical affliction, not all sickness is caused by demonic power.

Late hours did not keep Jesus from His appointed meeting with His Father early the next morning. Read Isaiah 50:4 for a prophetic description of God's righteous Servant as He meets the Father morning by morning. What an example for us to follow! It is no surprise that Jesus had such authority and power when His prayer life was so disciplined (see Mark 6:46; 9:28–29; 14:32–38).

However, the crowds wanted to see Jesus again, not to hear His word, but to experience His healing and see Him perform miracles. Peter was surprised that Jesus did not hasten to meet the crowds but instead left for other towns where He might preach the gospel. Peter did not realize the shallowness of the crowds, their unbelief, and their lack of appetite for the Word of God. Jesus said it was more important for Him to preach the gospel in other places than to stay there and heal the sick. He did not permit popular acclaim to change His priorities.

Perhaps we can understand our Lord's concern for a feverish woman, but that He would meet *and touch* a leper is somewhat beyond our understanding. Lepers were supposed to keep their distance and warn everyone that they were coming, lest others would be defiled (Lev. 13:45–46). This man knew that Jesus was *able* to heal him, but he was not sure the Master was *willing* to heal him. Lost sinners today have the same unnecessary concern, for God has made it abundantly clear that He is not willing that sinners perish (2 Peter 3:9) and that He is willing that all men be saved (1 Tim. 2:4).

When you read the "tests" for leprosy described in Leviticus 13, you can see how the disease is a picture of sin. Like sin, leprosy is deeper than the skin (Lev. 13:3); it spreads (Lev. 13:5–8); it defiles and isolates (Lev. 13:44–46); and it renders things fit only for the fire (Lev. 13:47–59). Anyone who has never trusted the Savior is spiritually in worse shape than this man was physically.

Jesus had compassion on the man (note Mark 6:34; 8:2; 9:22) and healed him. He did it with His touch and with His word. No doubt this was the first loving touch this leper had felt in a long time. As with the fever, so with the leprosy: It was gone instantly!

For reasons already stated, Jesus commanded the man not to tell everybody. He was to go to the priests and follow the instructions given in Leviticus 14, so that he might be declared clean and received back into the social and religious life of the community. However, the man disobeyed orders. Jesus told this man to keep quiet, and yet he told everybody. Jesus commands us to tell everybody—and we keep quiet! The crowds that came to get help from Jesus created a serious problem for Him and probably hindered Him from teaching the Word as He intended to (Mark 1:38).

The ceremony described in Leviticus 14 presents a beautiful picture in type of the work of redemption. The two birds represent two different aspects of our Lord's ministry: His incarnation and death (the bird put into the jar and then killed), and His resurrection and ascension (the bird stained with the blood and then set free). The blood was applied to the man's right ear (God's Word), right thumb (God's work), and right great toe (God's walk). Then the oil was put on the blood, symbolizing the Holy

Spirit of God. The Holy Spirit cannot come on human flesh until first the blood has been applied.

We should learn some important spiritual lessons from this chapter. To begin with, if the Son of God came as a servant, then being a servant is the highest of all callings. We are never more like the Lord Jesus than when we are serving others. Second, God shares His authority with His servants. Only those who are *under* authority have the right to *exercise* authority. Finally, if you are going to be a servant, be sure you have compassion, because people will come to you for help and rarely ask if it is convenient!

Yet, what a privilege it is to follow in the steps of Jesus Christ and meet the needs of others by being one of God's compassionate servants.

QUESTIONS FOR PERSONAL REFLECTION
OR GROUP DISCUSSION

1. What about Jesus' life shows you His servant spirit?

2. Why might the pagan Romans have struggled to accept that Jesus was the Son of God?

3. What does Mark tell us in chapter 1 about Jesus' identity? What evidence does he give to support this claim?

4. How did Jesus' baptism reflect His role as a servant?

5. List some ways in which Jesus' temptation reveals His servanthood.

6. What does a person's sense of authority reveal about his capacity to be a servant?

7. When Jesus expressed His authority over demons, what did the people watching learn about Him? How is this important for us?

8. When Jesus healed the people around Him of their illnesses, what did they learn of His servanthood? How is this important for us?

9. In what ways can we be servants like Jesus?

10. What role does compassion play in servanthood?

Chapter Two

WHAT THE SERVANT OFFERS YOU

(Mark 2:1—3:12)

With amazing speed the news spread that a miracle-working Teacher had come to Capernaum, and wherever our Lord went, great crowds gathered. They wanted to see Him heal the sick and cast out demons. Had they been interested in His message of the gospel, these multitudes would have been an encouragement to Jesus, but He knew that most of them were shallow in their thinking and blind to their own needs. Often the Lord found it necessary to leave the city and go out into the wilderness to pray (Luke 5:15–16). Every servant of God should follow His example and take time away from people in order to meet the Father and be refreshed and revitalized through prayer.

Now the time had come for Jesus to demonstrate to the people what His ministry was all about. After all, He had come to do much more than relieve the afflictions of the sick and the demonized. Those miracles were wonderful, but there was something greater for the people to experience—they could enter into the kingdom of God! They needed to understand the spiritual lessons that lay behind the physical miracles He was performing.

In this section, our Lord makes it clear that He came to bring to all who would trust Him three wonderful gifts: forgiveness (Mark 2:1–12), fulfillment (Mark 2:13–22), and freedom (Mark 2:23—3:12).

1. Forgiveness (2:1–12)

Whether this event took place in His own house ("He was at home" NASB) or Peter's house is not made clear. Since hospitality is one of the basic laws of the East, the people of Capernaum did not wait for an invitation but simply came to the house in droves. This meant that some of the truly needy people could not get close enough to Jesus to receive His help. However, four friends of a palsied man decided to lower their friend through the roof, trusting that Jesus would heal him, and Jesus did. This miracle of healing gave our Lord the opportunity to teach an important lesson about forgiveness.

Consider this scene through the eyes of the Lord Jesus. When He *looked up,* He saw the four men on the roof with their sick friend. Houses had flat roofs that were usually accessible by means of an outside stairway. It would not be difficult to remove the tiles, laths, and grass that comprised the roof and make an opening large enough to fit their friend through on his mat.

We must admire several characteristics of these men, qualities that ought to mark us as "fishers of men." For one thing, they were deeply concerned about their friend and wanted to see him helped. They had the faith to believe that Jesus could and would meet his need. They did not simply "pray about it," but they put some feet to their prayers, and they did not permit difficult circumstances to discourage them. They worked together and dared to do something different, and Jesus rewarded their efforts. How easy it would have been for them to say, "Well, there is no sense trying to get to Jesus today! Maybe we can come back tomorrow."

When our Lord *looked down,* He saw the palsied man lying on his mat, and immediately Jesus went to the heart of the man's problem—sin.

Not all sickness is caused by sin (see John 9:1–3), but evidently this man's condition was the result of his disobedience to God. Even before He healed the man's body, Jesus spoke peace to the man's heart and announced that his sins were forgiven! Forgiveness is the greatest miracle that Jesus ever performs. It meets the greatest need; it costs the greatest price; and it brings the greatest blessing and the most lasting results.

Then Jesus *looked around* and saw the critics who had come to spy on Him (see Luke 5:17). These religious leaders certainly had every right to investigate the ministry of this new teacher, since the religious life of the nation was under their supervision (Deut. 13). But they should have come with open minds and hearts, seeking truth, instead of with critical minds, seeking heresy. Some of the negative attitudes that had been present in Judea (John 4:1–4) had now invaded Galilee, and this was the beginning of the official opposition that ultimately led to our Lord's arrest and death. He was now so popular that the Jewish leaders dared not ignore Him. In fact, they must have arrived early for the meeting, because they were right at the scene of action! Or perhaps Jesus graciously gave them front row seats.

When the Lord *looked within,* He saw the critical spirit in their hearts and knew that they were accusing Him of blasphemy. After all, only *God* can forgive sins, and Jesus had just told the paralytic that his sins were forgiven. Jesus was claiming to be God!

But the next instant, He *proved* Himself to be God by reading their hearts and telling them what they were thinking (see John 2:25). Since they wanted to "reason" about things, He gave them something to ponder: Which is easier, to heal the man or to tell him he is forgiven? Obviously, it is easier to say, "Your sins are forgiven!" *because nobody can prove whether or not the forgiveness really took place.* So, to back up His words, Jesus immediately healed the man and sent him home. The healing of the man's body was but an illustration and demonstration of the healing of his soul

(Ps. 103:3). The scribes and Pharisees, of course, could neither heal the man nor forgive his sins, so they were caught in their own trap and condemned by their own thoughts.

Jesus affirmed His deity not only by forgiving the man's sins and healing his body, but also by applying to Himself the title "Son of man." This title is used fourteen times in Mark's gospel, and twelve of these references are found after Mark 8:29, when Peter confessed Jesus as the Christ of God (Mark 2:10, 28; 8:31, 38; 9:9, 12, 31; 10:33, 45; 13:26, 34; 14:21, 41, 62). It was definitely a messianic title (Dan. 7:13–14), and the Jews would have interpreted it that way. Jesus used this title about eighty times in the Gospels.

Suppose the religious leaders had opened their hearts to the truth that day, what could they have learned? For one thing, they could have learned that sin is like sickness and that forgiveness is like having your health restored. This was not a new truth, for the Old Testament Scriptures had said the same thing (Ps. 103:3; Isa. 1:5–6, 16–20); but now it had been demonstrated before their very eyes. They also could have learned that Jesus Christ of Nazareth is indeed the Savior with authority to forgive sins—and their own sins could have been forgiven! What an opportunity they missed when they came to the meeting with a critical spirit instead of with a repentant heart!

2. FULFILLMENT (2:13–22)

It soon became evident that Jesus was deliberately associating Himself with the outcasts of Jewish society. He even called a tax collector to become one of His disciples! We do not know that Levi was a dishonest man, though most of the tax collectors were, but the fact that he worked for Herod Antipas and the Romans was enough to disgrace him among loyal Jews. However, when Jesus called him, Levi did not argue or delay. He got up and followed Jesus, even though he knew that Rome would never give him back his job. He burned his bridges ("And he left everything behind,"

Luke 5:28 NASB), received a new name ("Matthew, the gift of God"), and enthusiastically invited some of his "sinner" friends to meet the Lord Jesus. These were Jewish people like himself who did not follow the law or appear to have much interest in religious things. They were exactly the kind of people Jesus wanted to reach.

Of course, the critics had to be there, but our Lord used their questions to teach the guests about Himself and the spiritual work He came to do. He explained His mission by using three interesting comparisons.

(1) The Physician (vv. 16–17). Jesus did not consider these people "rejects," even though they had been excommunicated by the religious leaders. Matthew's friends were *patients* who needed a physician, and Jesus was that Physician. We have already seen that sin may be compared to sickness and forgiveness to having your health restored. Now we see that our Savior may be compared to a physician: He comes to us in our need; He makes a perfect diagnosis; He provides a final and complete cure; and *He pays the bill!* What a physician!

But there are three kinds of "patients" whom Jesus cannot heal of their sin sickness: (1) those who do not know about Him; (2) those who know about Him but refuse to trust Him; and (3) those who will not admit that they need Him. The scribes and Pharisees were in that third category, as are all self-righteous sinners today. Unless we admit that we are sinners, deserving of God's judgment, we cannot be saved. Jesus saves only sinners (Luke 19:10).

In Jesus' day, as in the days of the prophets, there were those who claimed to bring spiritual healing to the people, but whose remedies were ineffective. Jeremiah rebuked the priests and false prophets of his day because they were worthless physicians who gave only a false hope to the nation. "They have healed also the hurt of the daughter of my people slightly, saying, 'Peace, peace'; when there is no peace" (Jer. 6:14; 8:11). They applied their weak medicines to the surface symptoms and did not get down deep into the basic problem—the sinful heart (Jer. 17:9). We must beware of such worthless physicians today.

(2) The Bridegroom (vv. 18–20). While the first question they asked had to do with the kind of company Jesus was keeping, their second question raised the issue of why Jesus was having such a good time with these people at the table. His conduct, to them, seemed inappropriate. John the Baptist was an austere man, somewhat of a recluse, but Jesus accepted invitations to meals, played with the children, and enjoyed social gatherings (Matt. 11:16–19). No doubt John's disciples were a bit scandalized to see Jesus at a party, and the pious disciples of the Pharisees (see Matt. 23:15) were quick to join them in their perplexity.

Jesus had already made it clear that He came to convert the sinners, not to compliment the self-righteous. Now He told them that He had come to bring gladness, not sadness. Thanks to the legalism imposed by the scribes and Pharisees, the Jewish religion had become a burdensome thing. The poor people were weighed down by rules and regulations that were impossible to obey (Matt. 23:4). "Life is not supposed to be a funeral!" Jesus told them. "God wants life to be a wedding feast! I am the Bridegroom and these people are my wedding guests. Are not wedding guests supposed to have a good time?"

The Jews knew that marriage was one of the pictures used in the Old Testament to help explain Israel's relationship to the Lord. They had been "married to Jehovah" and they belonged only to Him (Isa. 54:5; Jer. 31:32). When the nation turned to foreign gods, as they often did, they committed "spiritual adultery." They were unfaithful to their Husband, and they had to be disciplined. The major theme of Hosea is God's love for His adulterous wife and His desire to restore the nation to His favor once again.

John the Baptist had already announced that Jesus was the Bridegroom (John 3:29), and our Lord had performed His first miracle at a joyous marriage feast (John 2:1–11). Now He was inviting people to come to the wedding! After all, becoming a Christian is not unlike entering into the marriage relationship (see Rom. 7:4: "that ye should be married to another"). Two people are not married just because they know each other, or even because they have strong feelings about each other. In order to be married, they must commit themselves to each other and make this commitment known. In most societies, the man and woman publicly affirm this commitment when each says, "I do!"

Salvation from sin involves much more than a person knowing about Christ, or even having "good feelings" toward Christ. Salvation comes when the sinner commits himself or herself to Jesus Christ and says, "I do!" Then the believer immediately enters into the joys of this spiritual marriage relationship: bearing His name, sharing His wealth and power, enjoying His love and protection, and one day living in His glorious home in heaven. When you are "married to Christ," life becomes a wedding feast, in spite of trials and difficulties.

Mark 2:20 is a hint of our Lord's anticipated death, resurrection, and return to heaven. It is unlikely that His disciples, at that early stage in their training, even understood what He meant. However, Jesus was not suggesting that His absence from earth would mean that His followers would have to replace the feast with a funeral! He was only pointing out that occasional fasting would be proper at a future time, but that joyful celebration should be the normal experience of believers.

(3) The garment and the wineskins (vv. 21–22). Jesus taught two important lessons about His ministry: (1) He came to save sinners, not to call the religious; and (2) He came to bring gladness and not sadness. The third lesson is this: He came to introduce the new, not to patch up the old.

The religious leaders were impressed with our Lord's teaching, and perhaps they would have been happy to make some of His ideas a part of their own religious tradition. They were hoping for some kind of compromise that would retain the best of pharisaic Judaism and the best of what Christ had to offer. But Jesus exposed the folly of that approach. It would be like tearing patches from a new unshrunk garment and sewing them on an old garment. You would ruin the new garment, and when the old garment was washed, the patches would shrink, rip away, and ruin that garment too (note Luke 5:36–39). Or, it would be like putting new unfermented wine in old brittle wineskins. As soon as the wine began to ferment and the gases formed, the old skins would burst—and you would lose both the wine and the skins.

Jesus came to usher in the new, not to unite with the old. The Mosaic economy was decaying, getting old, and ready to vanish away (Heb. 8:13). Jesus would establish a new covenant in His blood (Luke 22:19–20). The law would be written on human hearts, not on stones (2 Cor. 3:1–3; Heb. 10:15–18), and the indwelling Holy Spirit would enable God's people to fulfill the righteousness of the law (Rom. 8:1–4).

By using this illustration, Jesus refuted once and for all the popular idea of a compromising "world religion." Well-meaning but spiritually blind leaders have suggested that we take "the best" from each religion, blend it with what is "best" in the Christian faith, and thus manufacture a synthetic faith that would be acceptable to everybody. But the Christian faith is *exclusive* in character; it will not accept any other faith as its equal or its superior. "There is none other name under heaven given among men, whereby we must be saved" (Acts 4:12).

Salvation is not a partial patching up of one's life; it is a whole new robe of righteousness (Isa. 61:10; 2 Cor. 5:21). The Christian life is not a mixing of the old and the new; rather, it is a fulfillment of the old in the new. There are two ways to destroy a thing: You can smash it or you can permit it to fulfill itself. An acorn, for example, can be smashed with a hammer, or it can be planted and allowed to grow into an oak. In both instances, the destruction of the acorn is accomplished, but in the second instance, the acorn is destroyed by being fulfilled.

Jesus fulfilled the prophecies, types, and demands of the law of Moses. The law was ended at Calvary when the perfect sacrifice was once offered for the sins of the world (Heb. 8—10). When you trust Jesus Christ, you become part of a new creation (2 Cor. 5:17), and there are always new experiences of grace and glory. How tragic when people hold on to dead religious tradition when they could lay hold of living spiritual truth. Why cherish the shadows when the reality has come (Heb. 10:1ff.)? In Jesus Christ we have the fulfillment of all that God promised (2 Cor. 1:20).

3. FREEDOM (2:23—3:12)

The Sabbath was cherished by the Jews as a sacred institution. God gave the people of Israel the Sabbath after they came out of Egypt (Ex. 20:8–11; Neh. 9:14), and it was a special sign between Israel and Jehovah (Ex. 31:13–17). There is no record in Scripture that God ever gave the Sabbath to any other nation. So, when Jesus began openly to violate the Sabbath traditions, it was like declaring war against the religious establishment. He began His campaign by healing a man who had been sick for thirty-eight years (John 5), and then followed with the events recorded in this section.

Jewish tradition stated that there were thirty-nine acts that were strictly forbidden on the Sabbath. Moses had prohibited work on the Sabbath, but he did not give many specifics (Ex. 20:10). It was wrong to kindle a fire for cooking (Ex. 35:3), gather fuel (Num. 15:32ff.), carry burdens (Jer. 17:21ff.), or transact business (Neh. 10:31; 13:15, 19). But Jewish tradition went into great detail and even informed the people how far they could travel on the Sabbath (two hundred cubits, based on Josh. 3:4). In short, the Sabbath day had become a crushing burden, a symbol of the galling religious bondage that had captured the nation.

After healing the man at the Pool of Bethesda, our Lord's next act of "Sabbath defiance" was to walk through the fields on the Sabbath and permit His disciples to pluck the grain, rub it between their hands, and eat it. It was not illegal for a hungry person to take some of his neighbor's fruit or grain, provided he did not fill a vessel or use a harvesting implement (Deut. 23:24–25). However, that was not what upset the Pharisees. What upset them was that the disciples had worked on the Sabbath day!

When you read Matthew's account of this event, you note that Jesus gave three arguments to defend His disciples: what David did (Matt. 12:3–4), what the priests did (Matt. 12:5–6), and what the prophet Hosea said (Matt. 12:7–8). Mark's Roman readers would not be interested in Jewish prophets and priests, so Mark focused on David, whom the Romans would recognize as a great hero and king. The argument is reasonable: If a hungry king and his men were permitted to eat the holy bread from the tabernacle (1 Sam. 21:1–6), then it was right for the Lord of the Sabbath to permit His men to eat the grain from His fields. David broke a definite law given by Moses, for the showbread was for the priests only (Lev. 24:5–9), but the disciples had violated only a man-made tradition. God is surely more concerned with meeting the needs of people than He is with protecting religious tradition. The Pharisees had their priorities confused.

Did Jesus make a mistake when He mentioned Abiathar as the high priest? The record in 1 Samuel 21 names Abimelech, the father of Abiathar (1 Sam. 22:20), as high priest, so our Lord's words appear to be a contradiction. They are not. It is possible that father and son each had both names (1 Chron. 18:16 and 24:6; 1 Sam. 22:20 and 2 Sam. 8:17). Also it is likely that our Lord used "Abiathar" to refer to the Old Testament *passage* about Abiathar rather than to the man. This is the way the Jews identified sections of the Word since their manuscripts did not have chapters and verses such as we have today in our Bibles (see Mark 12:26).

On that same Sabbath day, Jesus went into the synagogue to worship, and while He was there, He deliberately healed a man. Certainly He could have waited one more day, but once again He wanted to challenge the pharisaical legalistic traditions. This time the Pharisees (Luke 6:7) were expecting Him to heal, so they kept their eyes wide open. Our Lord's questions in Mark 3:4 were never answered by His enemies. Since *evil* is at work every day, including the Sabbath day, why should *good* not be at work as well? Death is always at work, but that should not hinder us from seeking to save life.

Jesus could see "the hardening of their hearts" (literal translation), and their sin made Him angry. Our Lord never became angry at the publicans and sinners, but He did express anger toward the self-righteous Pharisees (Matt. 23). They would rather protect their traditions than see a man healed! The man, of course, knew little about this spiritual conflict. He simply obeyed our Lord's command, stretched out his hand, and was healed.

So incensed were the Pharisees over what Jesus had done that they united with the Herodians and started making plans to arrest Jesus and destroy Him. The Herodians were not a religious party; they were a group of Jews who were sympathetic to King Herod and supported his rule. Most of the Jews despised Herod and obeyed his laws reluctantly, so it was surprising that the Pharisees, who were strict Jews, would join themselves with these disloyal politicians. But it was a common enemy—Jesus—that brought the two groups together.

In response to this united opposition, Jesus simply withdrew from there, but He could not prevent the great crowds from following Him. These crowds were dangerous to His cause, of course, because they were not spiritually motivated, and the authorities could accuse Him of leading a popular revolt against the Romans. Yet Jesus received the people, healed the sick, and delivered the demonized. Once again, He warned the demons not to reveal who He was (Mark 1:23–26).

Our Lord had now reached a crisis in His ministry. Great crowds were following Him, but their interest was not in things spiritual. The religious leaders wanted to destroy Him, and even some of Herod's friends were getting involved. His next step would be to spend a night in prayer (Luke 6:12), call twelve men to assist Him as His apostles, and preach a sermon—the Sermon on the Mount—explaining the spiritual basis of His kingdom.

He offered them forgiveness, fulfillment, and freedom, but they refused His offer.

Have *you* accepted His offer?

QUESTIONS FOR PERSONAL REFLECTION
OR GROUP DISCUSSION

1. What kinds of things hinder us from following Jesus' example of taking time for prayer? *Taking care of needs & chores for self, family & others.*

2. Name some things that prayer time accomplishes in our lives. *Refreshes our mind & soul. Rekindle our friendship w Jesus. Restores our hope*

3. What inspires you most about the account of the four men who lowered their friend through the roof so Jesus could heal him? *Their concern for their friend cemented their faith & friendship to meet his need.*

4. In this account, what relationship did Jesus' forgiving the man's sin have with healing his body? *If his sin (disobedience to God) caused his illness, he couldn't be healed without forgiveness.*

5. Jesus chose to befriend the unlovable. How can we practice this in our relationships? *We can contribute to causes which help those who cannot help themselves.*

6. List some ways that becoming a Christian is much like saying "I do" in a wedding ceremony. *you commit yourself to living according to Christ's example.*

7. What are the challenges of remembering that Jesus came to save sinners, not to please the righteous? *Some who felt righteous didn't realize they were really sinners. Some sinners couldn't believe the Good News.*

8. Wiersbe says, "Salvation is not a partial patching up of one's life; it is a whole new robe of righteousness." Describe what partially patching up one's life is like. *Jesus requires total committment or you are apt to fall back to old habits*

9. Jesus broke traditions such as not working on the Sabbath. Why do you think He felt free to do that? *Some chores or Emergencies can't wait. Jewish tradition (man-made) had become a Crushing burden*

10. In some ways Jesus was leading a rebellion against traditional religion. How would you describe Jesus' rebellion?

Evil is at work every day why should good not be?

Chapter Three

THE SERVANT, THE CROWDS, AND THE KINGDOM

(Mark 3:13—4:34)

No matter where He went, God's Servant was thronged by excited crowds (Mark 3:7–9, 20, 32; 4:1). Had Jesus been a "celebrity" and not a servant, He would have catered to the crowds and tried to please them (see Matt. 11:7–15). Instead, He withdrew from the crowds and began to minister especially to His disciples. Jesus knew that most of the people who pushed to get near Him were shallow and insincere, but His disciples did not know this. Lest they take all of this "success" seriously, Jesus had to teach these men the truth about the crowds and the kingdom. In this section, we see our Lord's three responses to the pressure of the crowd.

1. HE FOUNDED A NEW NATION (3:13–19)

The number of the disciples is significant because there were twelve tribes in the nation of Israel. In Genesis, God started with Jacob's twelve sons, and in Exodus, He built them into a mighty nation. Israel was chosen to bring the Messiah into the world so that through Him all the nations of the earth could be blessed (Gen. 12:1–3). However, the nation of Israel was now spiritually decayed and ready to reject her own Messiah. God had to establish "a holy nation, a peculiar [purchased] people" (1 Peter 2:9), and the twelve apostles were the nucleus of this new "spiritual" nation (Matt. 21:43).

Jesus spent all night in prayer before choosing these twelve men (Luke 6:12). When He selected them, He had three purposes in mind: (1) training them by personal example and teaching, (2) sending them out to preach the gospel, and (3) giving them authority to heal and cast out demons (see Mark 1:14–15, 38–39; 6:7–13). These twelve men would thus be able to continue His work when He returned to the Father, and they would also be able to train others to carry on the ministry after them (2 Tim. 2:2).

In the New Testament, you will find three other lists of the names of the twelve disciples: Matthew 10:2–4; Luke 6:14–16; and Acts 1:13. Luke tells us that Jesus gave them the special name "apostles." A "disciple" is one who learns by doing; our modern equivalent might be an "apprentice." An "apostle" is one who is sent on official service with a commission. Jesus had many disciples but only twelve apostles, His special "ambassadors."

When you compare the lists, it appears that the names are arranged in pairs: Peter and Andrew; James and John; Philip and Bartholomew (Nathanael [John 1:45]); Thomas and Matthew (Levi); James, the son of Alphaeus, and Thaddaeus (Judas, son of James, not Iscariot [John 14:22]); Simon the Zealot and Judas Iscariot. Since Jesus sent His apostles out two by two, this was a logical way to list them (Mark 6:7).

Simon's name was changed to Peter, "the rock" (John 1:40–42), and Levi's was changed to Matthew, "the gift of God." James and John were given the nicknames, "Boanerges—the sons of thunder." We commonly think of John as the apostle of love, but he certainly did not begin with that kind of reputation, nor did James his brother (Mark 9:38–41; 10:35–39; Luke 9:54–55). It is encouraging to see what Jesus was able to do with such a diversified group of unlikely candidates for Christian service. There is still hope for us!

Mark defined the Hebrew word *Boanerges* because he was writing for Roman readers. In his gospel you will find several of these "special notes for Gentiles" (Mark 5:41; 7:11, 34; 11:9; 14:36; 15:22, 34). The word *Canaanite* in Mark 3:18 has nothing to do with national or racial origin. It is the Hebrew word *cananaean,* which comes from a word that means "to be jealous, to be zealous." The Zealots were a group of Jewish extremists organized to overthrow Rome, and they used every means available to advance their cause. The historian Josephus called them "daggermen." It would be interesting to know how Simon the Zealot responded when he first met Matthew, a former employee of Rome.

If you consult a harmony of the Gospels, you will see that between Mark 3:19 and 20, Jesus preached the Sermon on the Mount (Matt. 5—7) and participated in the events described in Luke 7:1—8:3. Mark's gospel does not include that famous sermon because his emphasis is on what Jesus did rather than what Jesus said.

2. He Established a New Family (3:20–21, 31–35)

Our Lord's friends were sure that Jesus was confused, and possibly deranged! The great crowds they saw following Him, and the amazing reports they heard about Him, convinced them that He desperately needed help. He simply was not living a normal life, so His friends came to Capernaum to "take charge of him." Then his mother and "brethren" (Mark 6:3) traveled thirty miles from Nazareth to plead with Him to come home and get some rest, but even they were unable to get near Him. This is the only place in the gospel of Mark where Mary is seen, and her venture was a failure.

History reveals that God's servants are usually misjudged by their contemporaries, and often misunderstood by their families. D. L. Moody was called "Crazy Moody" by many people in Chicago, and even the great apostle Paul was called mad (Acts 26:24–25). Emily Dickinson wrote:

Much madness is divinest sense
To a discerning eye;
Much sense the starkest madness.
'Tis the majority
In this, as all, prevails.
Assent, and you are sane;
Demur—you're straightway dangerous,
And handled with a chain.

Our Lord was not being rude to His family when He remained in the house and did not try to see them. He knew that their motives were right but their purpose was definitely wrong. If Jesus had yielded to His family, He would have played right into the hands of the opposition. The religious leaders would have said, "See, He agreed with His family—He needs help! Don't take Jesus of Nazareth too seriously." Instead of giving in, He used this crisis as an opportunity to teach a spiritual lesson: His "family" is made up of all those who do the will of God. Our Lord's half-brothers were not believers (John 7:1–5), and Jesus felt closer to the believing publicans and sinners than He did to James, Joses, Judah, and Simon, His half-brothers.

Our Lord was not suggesting that believers ignore or abandon their families in order to serve God, but only that they put God's will above everything else in life. Our love for God should be so great that our love for family would seem like hatred in comparison (Luke 14:26). Certainly it is God's will that we care for our families and provide for them (see 1 Tim. 5:8), but we must not permit even our dearest loved ones to influence us away from the will of God. When you consider the importance of the family in the Jewish society, you can imagine how radical Christ's words must have sounded to those who heard them.

How does one enter into the family of God? By means of a new birth, a spiritual birth from above (John 3:1–7; 1 Peter 1:22–25). When the sinner trusts Jesus Christ as Savior, he experiences this new birth and enters into God's family. He shares God's divine nature (2 Peter 1:3–4) and can call God "Father" (Rom. 8:15–16). This spiritual birth is not something that we accomplish for ourselves, nor can others do it for us (John 1:11–13). It is God's work of grace; all we can do is believe and receive (Eph. 2:8–9).

3. He Announced a New Kingdom (3:22–30; 4:1–34)

The crowds hoped that Jesus would deliver the nation and defeat Rome. Instead, He called twelve ordinary men and founded a "new nation," a spiritual nation whose citizens had their names written down in heaven (Luke 10:20; Phil. 3:20). The crowds wanted Jesus to behave like a loyal Jew and honor His family, but Jesus established a "new family" made up of all those who trusted Him and did the will of God. The crowds also expected Him to restore the kingdom and bring back Israel's lost glory, but His response was to announce a new kingdom, a spiritual kingdom.

"Kingdom" is a key word in this section (Mark 3:24; 4:11, 26, 30). John the Baptist had announced that the arrival of the King was near, and he had warned the people to prepare to meet Him (Mark 1:1–8). Jesus took up John's message and preached the good news of the kingdom and the necessity for sinners to repent and believe (Mark 1:14–15). But what is this kingdom like? If the Lord was not going to restore Israel and set up a political kingdom, what kind of kingdom was He planning to establish?

At this point, Mark introduced a new word—*parables* (see Mark 3:23; 4:2, 10–11, 13, 33–34). Jesus explained the kingdom, not by giving a lecture on theology, but by painting pictures that captured the attention of the people and forced them to use their imaginations and think. Our

English word *parable* comes from two Greek words that mean "to cast alongside" (*para*—alongside; *ballo*—to throw or cast). A parable is a story or figure placed alongside a teaching to help us understand its meaning. It is much more than "an earthly story with a heavenly meaning," and it certainly is not an "illustration" such as a preacher would use in a sermon. A true parable gets the listener deeply involved and compels that listener to make a personal decision about God's truth and his or her life. So penetrating and personal are parables that, after they heard several of them, the religious leaders wanted to kill the Lord Jesus! (See Matt. 21:45–46.)

A parable begins innocently as a *picture* that arrests our attention and arouses our interest. But as we study the picture, it becomes a *mirror* in which we suddenly see ourselves. If we continue to look by faith, the mirror becomes a *window* through which we see God and His truth. How we respond to that truth will determine what further truth God will teach us.

Why did Jesus teach in parables? His disciples asked Him that very question (Mark 4:10–12; see Matt. 13:10–17). A careful study of His reply reveals that Jesus used parables both to hide the truth and to reveal it. The crowd did not judge the parables; the parables judged the crowd. The careless listener, who thought he knew everything, would hear only a story that he did not really understand, and the result in his life would be judgment (see Matt. 11:25–30). The sincere listener, with a desire to know God's truth, would ponder the parable, confess his ignorance, submit to the Lord, and then begin to understand the spiritual lesson Jesus wanted to teach.

Jesus placed a great deal of importance on the *hearing of the Word of God*. In one form or another, the word *hear* is used thirteen times in Mark 4:1–34. Obviously, our Lord was speaking, not about physical hearing, but about hearing with spiritual discernment. To "hear" the Word of God means to understand it and obey it (see James 1:22–25).

Our Lord gave several parables to help the people (and that included His disciples) understand the nature of His kingdom.

The strong man (3:22–30). Jesus healed a demoniac who was both blind and mute (Matt. 12:22–24), and the scribes and Pharisees used this miracle as an opportunity to attack Him. The crowd was saying, "Perhaps this Man is indeed the Son of David, the Messiah." But the religious leaders said, "No, He is in league with Beelzebub! It is Satan's power that is at work in Him, not God's power."

"Beelzebub" (or "Beelzebul") is a name for the Devil, and it means "master of the house." Jesus picked up on this meaning and gave a parable about a strong man guarding his house. To plunder the house, one must first overcome the strong man.

Jesus exposed both their bad theology and their faulty logic. If it was by the power of Satan that He had cast out the demon, then Satan was actually fighting against himself! This meant that Satan's house and kingdom were divided and therefore on the verge of collapse. Satan had been guarding that man carefully because the Devil does not want to lose any of his territory. The fact that Jesus delivered the man was proof that He was stronger than Satan and that Satan could not stop Him.

Jesus did much more than answer their false accusation. He went on to explain the seriousness of what they had said. After all, our words reveal what is hidden in our hearts (Matt. 12:35), and what is in our hearts determines our character, conduct, and destiny. We sometimes say, "Talk is cheap!" But in reality, what we say can be very costly. Jesus warned the Jewish religious leaders that they were in danger of committing an eternal and unforgivable sin (Matt. 12:32).

When you ask people, "What is the unpardonable sin?" they usually reply, "It is blaspheming the Holy Spirit" or "It is the sin of attributing to the Devil the works of the Holy Spirit." Historically speaking, these statements are true, but they do not really answer the question. How do we *today* blaspheme the Spirit of God? What miracles is the Holy Spirit performing *today* that might be carelessly or even deliberately attributed to Satan? Must a person see a miracle in order to commit this terrible sin?

Jesus made it clear that God would forgive *all* sin and *all* blasphemy, *including blasphemy against the very Son of God Himself* (Matt. 12:32)! Does this mean that God the Son is less important than the Holy Spirit? Why would a sin against God the Son be forgivable and yet a sin against the Holy Spirit be unforgivable?

The answer lies in the nature of God and in His patient dealings with the nation of Israel. God the Father sent John the Baptist to prepare the nation for the coming of their Messiah. Many of the common people responded to John's call and repented (Matt. 21:32), but the religious leaders *permitted* John to be arrested and eventually killed. God the Son came as promised and called the nation to trust Him, but those same religious leaders *asked for* Jesus to be killed. On the cross, our Lord prayed, "Father, forgive them; for they know not what they do" (Luke 23:34).

The Holy Spirit came at Pentecost and demonstrated God's power in many convicting ways. How did those same religious leaders respond? By arresting the apostles, ordering them to keep silent, and then *killing Stephen themselves!* Stephen told them what their sin was: "Ye do always resist the Holy Ghost" (Acts 7:51). They had sinned against the Father and the Son, but had been graciously forgiven. When they sinned against the Holy Spirit, they had reached "the end of the line," and there could be no more forgiveness.

People today cannot commit the "unpardonable sin" in the same way the Jewish religious leaders did when Jesus was ministering on earth. The only sin today that God cannot forgive is rejection of His Son (John 3:16–21, 31). When the Spirit of God convicts the sinner and reveals the Savior, the sinner may resist the Spirit and reject the witness of the Word of God, but that does not mean he has forfeited all his opportunities to be saved. If he will repent and believe, God can still forgive him. Even if the sinner so hardens his heart that he seems to be insensitive to the pleadings of God, so long as there is life, there is hope. Only God knows if and when any "deadline" has been crossed. You and I must never despair of any sinner (1 Tim. 2:4; 2 Peter 3:9).

The sower and the soils (4:1–20). This parable helped the disciples understand why Jesus was not impressed by the large crowds that followed Him. He knew that most of them would never produce fruit from changed lives, because the Word He was teaching them was like seed falling into poor soil.

The seed represents God's Word (Luke 8:11), and the sower is the servant of God who shares that Word with others (see 1 Cor. 3:5–9). The human heart is like soil: It must be prepared to receive the seed before that seed can take root and produce a harvest. Like seed, the Word is alive and able to produce spiritual fruit, but the seed must be planted and cultivated before that harvest will come. As in that day, so today, there are four kinds of hearts, and they respond to God's message in four different ways.

1. *The hard heart (Mark 4:4, 15)* resists the Word of God and makes it easy for Satan (the birds) to snatch it away. Soil becomes hard when too many feet tread on it. Those who recklessly "open their hearts" to all kinds of people and influences are in danger of developing hard hearts (see Prov. 4:23). Hard hearts must be "plowed up" before they can receive the seed, and this can be a painful experience (Jer. 4:3; Hos. 10:12).

2. *The shallow heart (vv. 5–6, 16–17)* is like thin soil on a rock, very typical to Palestine. Since there is no depth, whatever is planted cannot last because it has no roots. This represents the "emotional hearer" who joyfully accepts God's Word but does not really understand the price that must be paid to become a genuine Christian. There may be great enthusiasm for several days or weeks, but when persecution and difficulties begin, the enthusiasm wanes and the joy disappears. It is easy for fallen human nature

to counterfeit "religious feelings" and give a professed Christian a feeling of false confidence.

3. *The crowded heart* (vv. 7, 18–19) pictures the person who receives the Word but does not truly repent and remove the "weeds" out of his or her heart. This hearer has too many different kinds of "seeds" growing in the soil—worldly cares, a desire for riches, a lust for things—and the good seed of the Word has no room in which to grow. To change the image, this person wants to walk the "broad way" and the "narrow way" at the same time (Matt. 7:13–14) and it cannot be done.

4. *The fruitful heart* (vv. 8, 20) pictures the true believer, because fruit—a changed life—is the evidence of true salvation (2 Cor. 5:17; Gal. 5:19–23). The other three hearts produced no fruit, so we conclude that they belong to persons who have never been born again. Not all true believers are equally as productive, but from every genuine Christian's life, there will be some evidence of spiritual fruit.

Each of the three fruitless hearts is influenced by a different enemy: the hard heart—the Devil himself snatches the seed; the shallow heart—the flesh counterfeits religious feelings; the crowded heart—the things of the world smother the growth and prevent a harvest. These are the three great enemies of the Christian: the world, the flesh, and the Devil (Eph. 2:1–3).

The lamp (4:21–25). In this parable, our Lord used a common object (a lamp) in a familiar scene (a home). The lamp was a clay dish filled with oil, with a wick put into the oil. In order to give light, the lamp had to "use itself up," and the oil had to be replenished. If the lamp was not lit, or if it was covered up, it did the home no good.

The apostles were like that lamp: They were called to shed God's light and reveal His truth. But they could not "give out" without first "taking in"; hence the admonition of Mark 4:24–25. The more we hear the Word of God, the better we are able to share it with others. The moment we think that we know it all, what we think we know will be taken from us.

We must take heed *what* we hear (Mark 4:24) as well as take heed *how* we hear (Luke 8:18). Our spiritual hearing determines how much we have to give to others. There is no sense trying to "cover things up" because God will one day reveal all things.

The seed growing (4:26–34). The first parable reminds us that we cannot make the seed grow; in fact, we cannot even explain *how* it grows. There is a mystery to the growth of the seed and the development of the harvest. It takes a good deal of faith to be a farmer, and also a good deal of patience. In the parable of the sower and the soils, the Lord suggested that much of the seed scattered would fall on unproductive soil. This fact could discourage His workers, so in this parable He reassured them "in due season we shall reap, if we faint not" (Gal. 6:9).

The second parable gave the disciples both warning and encouragement. The encouragement was that, from very small beginnings, the kingdom would eventually grow in size and in influence. While a mustard seed is not the smallest seed in the world, it was probably the smallest seed that the Jews sowed in their gardens. It was a traditional symbol of that which is tiny. Our Lord began with twelve apostles. Later, there were as many as five hundred believers (1 Cor. 15:6). Peter won three thousand at Pentecost, and throughout the book of Acts, that number steadily increased (Acts 4:4; 5:14; 6:1, 7). In spite of the sins and weaknesses of the church, the message has been carried to other nations, and one day, saints from *every* nation shall worship before His throne (Rev. 5:9).

But the growth of the seed is only one part of the story; we must also account for the birds in the branches. In the parable of the sower and soils, the birds stood for Satan, who snatches the seed (Mark 4:15). If we are to be consistent in our interpretation, we must take this into consideration, for both parables were taught on the same day. The growth of the kingdom will not result in the conversion of the world. In fact, some of the growth will give opportunity for Satan to get in and go to work! There was Judas in the disciple band, and Ananias and Sapphira were in fellowship with the Jerusalem church (Acts 5:1–11). Simon Magus was part of the church in Samaria (Acts 8:9–24), and Satan's ministers boldly invaded the Corinthian church (2 Cor. 11:13–15). The bigger the net, the greater the possibility of catching both good and bad fish (Matt. 13:47–50).

Through faith in Jesus Christ, we become citizens of the heavenly nation, children in God's family, and subjects of the King of Kings and Lord of Lords. What a privilege it is to know the Lord Jesus Christ!

QUESTIONS FOR PERSONAL REFLECTION
OR GROUP DISCUSSION

1. List some of the differences between being a celebrity and being a servant. *celebrites cater to the crowds & try to please them. servants care about a person's change of heart.*

2. What do you think made the disciples respond to Jesus and walk away from their lives? *Jesus had an appeal to a variety of persons. This is a good example for us today. God uses ordinary people for extraordinary purposes.*

3. If becoming a Christian is like becoming a part of a new family, what responsibilities go along with that? *Believers are expected to put God's will above every thing else. Spiritual birth is God's work of grace.*

4. The Jews of Jesus' day thought that He was coming to set up a political kingdom. Describe the kind of kingdom that Jesus came to set up instead.

5. Name some reasons that the religious leaders of Jesus' day were so threatened by His popularity.

6. Why were parables a powerful way for Jesus to teach?

7. To which of the seeds/hearts in the parable of the sower would you compare your faith? Are you more of a hard heart, a shallow heart, a crowded heart, or a fruitful heart? What makes you think that?

8. List some ways that our lives are like the oil lamp in Jesus' parable in Mark 4:21.

9. Describe a time when you saw something happen that you believe was Satan moving against the work of Christ.

10. How do you think Jesus would invite someone, in today's language, to join God's family?

Chapter Four

THE SERVANT CONQUERS!

(Mark 4:35—5:43)

God's Servant, Jesus Christ, is the Master of every situation and the Conqueror of every enemy. If we trust Him and follow His orders, we need never be afraid. *Victory* is the major theme that binds this long section together. Mark recorded four miracles that Jesus performed, and each miracle announces even to us today the defeat of an enemy.

1. VICTORY OVER DANGER (4:35–41)

"The same day" refers to the day on which Jesus gave the "parables of the kingdom." He had been teaching His disciples the Word, and now He would give them a practical test to see how much they had really learned. After all, the hearing of God's Word is intended to produce faith (Rom. 10:17), and faith must always be tested. It is not enough for us merely to learn a lesson or be able to repeat a teaching. We must also be able to practice that lesson by faith, and that is one reason why God permits trials to come to our lives.

Did Jesus know that the storm was coming? Of course He did! The storm was a part of that day's curriculum. It would help the disciples understand a lesson that they did not even know they needed to learn: Jesus can be trusted in the storms of life. Many people have the idea that storms come to their lives only when they have disobeyed God, but this is not always the case. Jonah ended up in a storm because of his disobedience, but the disciples got into a storm because of their *obedience* to the Lord.

The geographic location of the Sea of Galilee is such that sudden violent storms are not unusual. While crossing this very sea one summer afternoon, I asked an Israeli tour guide if he had ever been in such a storm. "I certainly have!" he replied, throwing up his hands and shaking his head. "And I never want to be in one like it again!"

The storm described here must have been especially fierce if it frightened experienced fishermen like the disciples. There were at least three good reasons why none of the men in the ship should have been disturbed, even though the situation appeared to be threatening.

1. To begin with, they had His promise that they were going to the other side (Mark 4:35). His commandments are always His enablements, and nothing can hinder the working out of His plans. He did not promise an easy trip, but He did promise a guaranteed arrival at their destination.

2. Second, the Lord Himself was with them, so what was there to fear? They had already seen His power demonstrated in His miracles, so they should have had complete confidence that He could handle the situation. For some reason, the disciples did not yet understand that He was indeed the Master of every situation.

3. Finally, they could see that Jesus was perfectly at peace, even in the midst of the storm. This fact alone should have encouraged them. Jesus was in God's will and knew that the Father would care for Him, so He took a nap. Jonah slept during a storm because he had a false sense of security, even though he was running from God. Jesus slept in the storm because He was truly secure in God's will. "I will both lay me down in peace, and sleep for thou, LORD, only makest me dwell in safety" (Ps. 4:8).

How often in the trials of life we are prone to imitate the faithless disciples and cry out, "Lord, don't You care?" Of course, He cares! He arose and rebuked the storm, and immediately there was a great calm. But Jesus did not stop with the calming of the elements, for the greatest danger was not the wind or the waves, it was the unbelief in the hearts of the disciples. Our greatest problems are within us, not around us. This explains why Jesus gently rebuked them and called them "men of little faith." They had heard Him teach the Word and had even seen Him perform miracles, and yet they still had no faith. It was their unbelief that caused their fear, and their fear made them question whether Jesus really cared. We must beware of "an evil heart of unbelief" (Heb. 3:12).

This was only one of many lessons Jesus would teach His disciples in the familiar environs of the Sea of Galilee, and each lesson would reveal some wonderful new truth about the Lord Jesus. They already knew that He had the authority to forgive sins, to cast out demons, and to heal diseases. Now they discovered that He even had authority over the wind and the sea. This meant that they had no reason ever again to be afraid, for their Lord was in constant control of every situation.

2. Victory over Demons (5:1–20)

When Jesus and the disciples landed on the other side, they encountered two demoniacs, one of whom was especially vocal (see Matt. 8:28). This entire scene seems very unreal to us who live in so-called "modern civilization," but it would not be unreal in many mission fields. In fact, some Bible teachers believe that demon possession is becoming even more prevalent in today's "modern society."

We see in this scene three different forces at work: Satan, society, and the Savior. These same three forces are still at work in our world, trying to control the lives of people.

First, we see what *Satan* can do to people. Satan is a thief whose ultimate purpose is to destroy (John 10:10; and see Rev. 9:11). We are not told how the demons entered these men and took control, but possibly it was the result of their yielding to sin. Demons are "unclean spirits" and can easily get a foothold in the lives of people who cultivate sinful practices.

Because they yielded to Satan, the thief, these two men lost everything! They lost their homes and the fellowship of their families and friends. They lost their decency as they ran around in the tombs naked. They lost their self-control and lived like wild animals, screaming, cutting themselves, and frightening the citizens. They lost their peace and their purpose for living, and they would have remained in that plight had Jesus not come through a storm to rescue them.

Never underestimate the destructive power of Satan. He is our enemy and would destroy all of us if he could. Like a roaring lion, he seeks to devour us (1 Peter 5:8–9). It is Satan who is at work in the lives of unbelievers, making them "children of disobedience" (Eph. 2:1–3). The two men in the Gerasene graveyard were no doubt extreme examples of what Satan can do to people, but what they reveal is enough to make us want to resist Satan and have nothing to do with him.

The second force at work on these men was *society*, but society was not able to accomplish very much. About all that society can do for problem people is to isolate them, put them under guard and, if necessary, bind them (Luke 8:29). Often these men were chained, but the demons gave them strength to break the chains. Even the attempts to tame these men had failed. With all of its wonderful scientific achievements, society still cannot cope with the problems caused by Satan and sin. While we thank God that society does offer a limited amount of restraint and protection, we must confess that society cannot permanently solve these problems and deliver Satan's terrorized victims.

This brings us to the third force, that of the *Savior*. What did Jesus Christ do for these men? To begin with, He graciously came to them in love, and even went through a storm to do it. Some think that the storm itself may have been satanic in origin, since Jesus used the same words to calm the sea as He did to cast out demons (compare Mark 1:25 and 4:39). Perhaps Satan was trying to destroy Jesus, or at least prevent Him from coming to the men who needed Him. But nothing could stop the Lord from coming to that graveyard and bringing deliverance to those men.

Not only did Jesus come to them, but He spoke to them and permitted them to speak to Him. The citizens of that area avoided the two demoniacs, but Jesus treated them with love and respect. He came "to seek and to save that which was lost" (Luke 19:10).

It is interesting to note that, as the demons spoke through the man, they confessed what they really believed. Demons have faith and even tremble because of what they believe (James 2:19), but neither their faith nor their fear can save them. Demons believe that Jesus is the Son of God and that He has authority over them. They believe in the reality of judgment and that one day they will be cast into hell (see Matt. 8:29). This is more than many religious people believe today!

Nowhere does the Bible explain either the psychology or the physiology of demon possession. The man who spoke to Jesus was under the control of a *legion* of demons, and a Roman legion could consist of as many as six thousand men! It is frightening to think of the horrors this man experienced day and night as thousands of unclean spirits tormented him. No doubt the other demonized man experienced his share of agony too.

Satan tried to destroy these men, but Jesus came to deliver them. By the power of His word, He cast out the demons and set the men free. Demons even believe in prayer, for they begged Jesus not to send them into the abyss, the place of torment (Mark 5:7; Luke 8:31). It is encouraging to note that the demons did not know what Jesus planned to do. This suggests that Satan can know God's plans only if God reveals them. In fact, there is no evidence in Scripture that Satan can read the mind of a believer, let alone the mind of God.

Mark 5 tells of three requests: (1) The demons requested that Jesus send them into the pigs (Mark 5:12); (2) the citizens requested that Jesus leave the area (Mark 5:17); and (3) one of the former demoniacs requested that Jesus allow him to follow Him (Mark 5:18). Our Lord granted the first two requests but not the third one.

Did Jesus have the right to destroy two thousand pigs and possibly put their owners out of business? If these men were Jews, then they had no right to be raising and selling unclean pigs anyway. However, this was Gentile territory, so the owners were probably Gentiles.

Certainly, Jesus was free to send the demons wherever He desired—into the abyss, into the swine, or to any other place that He chose. Then why send them into the swine? For one thing, by doing it that way, Jesus gave proof to all the spectators that a miracle of deliverance had really taken place. The destruction of the pigs also gave assurance to the two men that the unclean spirits were actually gone. But more than anything else, the drowning of the two thousand swine was a vivid object lesson to this Christ-rejecting crowd that, to Satan, a pig is as good as a man! In fact, Satan will make a man into a pig! The Lord was warning the citizens against the powers of sin and Satan. It was a dramatic sermon before their very eyes: "The wages of sin is death!"

The swineherds did not want to be blamed for the loss of the pigs, so they immediately ran to tell the owners what had happened. When the owners arrived at the scene, they were afraid as they beheld the dramatic changes that had taken place in the two men. Instead of running around naked, the men were clothed, seated, and in their right minds. They were new creatures (2 Cor. 5:17)!

Why would the owners ask Jesus to leave? Why not ask Him to stay and perform similar cures for others who were also in need? The owners had one main interest—business—and they were afraid that if Jesus remained any longer, He would do even more "damage" to the local economy! Our Lord does not stay where He is not wanted, so He left. What an opportunity these people missed!

Why did Jesus not permit the healed demoniac to follow Him? The man's request was certainly motivated by love for the Lord Jesus, and what a testimony he had! But Jesus knew that the man's place was in his own home, with his loved ones, where he could bear witness to the Savior. After all, effective Christian living must begin at home, where people know us the best. If we honor God there, then we can consider offering ourselves for service elsewhere. This man became one of the earliest missionaries to the Gentiles. Jesus had to leave, but the man remained and bore faithful witness to the grace and power of Jesus Christ. We trust that many of those Gentiles believed on the Savior through his witness.

3. VICTORY OVER DISEASE (5:21–34)

One crowd sighed with relief as they saw Jesus leave, but another crowd was waiting to welcome Him when He returned home to Capernaum. In that latter crowd stood two people who were especially anxious to see Him—Jairus, a man with a dying daughter; and an anonymous woman suffering from an incurable disease. It was Jairus who approached Jesus first, but it was the woman who was first helped, so we shall begin with her.

The contrast between these two needy people is striking and reveals the wideness of Christ's love and mercy. Jairus was an important synagogue officer, and the woman was an anonymous "nobody," yet Jesus welcomed and helped both of them. Jairus was about to lose a daughter who had given him twelve years of happiness (Mark 5:42), and the woman was about to lose an affliction that had brought her twelve years of sorrow.

Being a synagogue officer, Jairus was no doubt wealthy, but his wealth could not save his dying daughter. The woman was already bankrupt! She had given the doctors all of her money, and yet none of them could cure her. Both Jairus and the poor woman found the answers to their needs at the feet of Jesus (Mark 5:22, 33).

The woman had a hemorrhage that was apparently incurable and was slowly destroying her. One can only imagine the pain and emotional pressure that sapped her strength day after day. When you consider her many disappointments with the doctors and the poverty it brought her, you wonder how she endured as long as she did. But there was one added burden: According to the law, she was ceremonially unclean, which greatly restricted both her religious and her social life (Lev. 15:19ff.). What a burden she carried!

However, she let nothing stand in her way as she pushed through the crowd and came to Jesus. She could have used any number of excuses to convince herself to stay away from Him. She might have said, "I'm not important enough to ask Jesus for help!" or "Look, He's going with Jairus, so I won't bother Him now." She could have argued that nothing else had helped her, so why try again? Or she might have concluded that it was not right to come to Jesus as a last resort, after visiting all those physicians. However, she laid aside all arguments and excuses and came by faith to Jesus.

What kind of faith did she have? It was weak, timid, and perhaps somewhat superstitious. She kept saying to herself that she had to touch His clothes in order to be healed (see Mark 3:10; 6:56). She had heard reports of others being healed by Jesus (Mark 5:27), so she made this one great attempt to get through to the Savior. She was not disappointed: Jesus honored her faith, weak as it was, and healed her body.

There is a good lesson here for all of us. Not everybody has the same degree of faith, but Jesus responds to faith no matter how feeble it might be. When we believe, He shares His power with us and something happens in our lives. There were many others in that crowd who were close to Jesus and even pressing against Him, but they experienced no miracles. Why? Because they did not have faith. It is one thing to throng Him and quite something else to trust Him.

The woman planned to slip away and get lost in the crowd, but Jesus turned and stopped her. Tenderly, He elicited from her a wonderful testimony of what the Lord had done for her. Why did Jesus deal with her publicly? Why did He not simply permit her to remain anonymous and go her way?

For one thing, He did it for her own sake. He wanted to be to her something more than a healer: He wanted to be her Savior and Friend as well. He wanted her to look into His face, feel His tenderness, and hear His loving words of assurance. By the time He finished speaking to her, she experienced something more than physical healing. He called her "daughter" and sent her on her way with a benediction of peace (Mark 5:34). To "be made whole" meant much more than receiving mere physical healing. Jesus had given her spiritual healing as well!

He dealt with her publicly not only for her sake, but also for the sake of Jairus. His daughter was close to death, and he needed all the encouragement he could get. It was bad enough that the crowd was impeding their progress, but now this woman had to interfere and stop Jesus! When one of Jairus's friends arrived and announced that the girl had died, no doubt Jairus felt that the end had come. The Lord's words to the woman about faith and peace must have encouraged Jairus as much as they encouraged her.

Finally, Jesus dealt with her publicly that she might have the opportunity to share her testimony and glorify the Lord. "Let the redeemed of the LORD say so, whom he hath redeemed from the hand of the enemy.... He sent his word, and healed them.... Oh, that men would praise the LORD for his goodness, and for his wonderful works to the children of men!"

(Ps. 107:2, 20–21). No doubt some people in that crowd heard her words and trusted in the Savior, and when she arrived home, she already knew what it meant to witness for Christ.

4. Victory over Death (5:35–43)

It was not easy for Jairus to come to Jesus publicly and ask for His help. The religious leaders who were opposed to Jesus would certainly not approve, nor would some of the other synagogue leaders. The things that Jesus had done and taught in the synagogues had aroused the anger of the scribes and Pharisees, some of whom were probably Jairus's friends. But Jairus was desperate, as many people are when they come to Jesus. He would rather lose his friends and save his beloved daughter.

It is beautiful to watch Jesus deal with Jairus and lead him to joyful victory. Throughout this entire event, it was our Lord's *words* that made the difference. Consider the three statements that He made.

(1) The word of faith (v. 36). At this point, Jairus had to believe either his friend or the Lord Jesus. No doubt all of his being responded with convulsive sorrow when he heard that his beloved daughter was dead. But Jesus assured him, "Be not afraid, go on believing" (literal translation). In other words, "You had a certain amount of faith when you came to Me, and your faith was helped when you saw what I did for that woman. Don't quit! Keep on believing!"

It was easier for Jairus to trust the Lord while his daughter was still alive, and while Jesus was still walking with him to his house. But when Jesus stopped to heal the woman, and when the friend came with the bad news, Jairus just about lost his faith. Let's not be too hard on him. We have probably given way to doubts when circumstances and feelings have overwhelmed us. Sometimes God has delayed, and we have wondered why. That is when we need that special "word of faith" from the Lord, and we receive it as we spend time in His Word.

(2) The word of hope (v. 39). When Jesus and Jairus arrived at the house, they saw and heard the professional Jewish mourners who were always summoned when a death occurred. It was traditional for them to wail loudly, to weep, and to lead the family and friends in lamentation. The presence of the mourners in the home is proof that the girl was actually dead, for the family would not have called them if there had been even the slightest hope that the girl was still alive.

"The child is not dead but sleeps!" were our Lord's words of hope to Jairus and his wife. To the believer, death is only sleep, for the body rests until the moment of resurrection (1 Thess. 4:13–18). The spirit does not sleep, for in death, the spirit of the believer leaves the body (James 2:26) and goes to be with Christ (Phil. 1:20–23). It is the body that sleeps, awaiting the return of the Lord and the resurrection (1 Cor. 15:51–58). This truth is a great encouragement to all of us who have had Christian loved ones and friends depart in death. It is His word of hope to us.

(3) The word of love and power (v. 41). Unbelief laughs at God's Word, but faith lays hold of it and experiences the power of God. Jesus did not make a spectacle of this miracle. He was sensitive to the feelings of the parents and grieved by the scornful attitude of the mourners. *Talitha cumi* is Aramaic for "Little girl, get up!" Jesus added, "I say unto thee" (with the emphasis on the *I),* because it was by His authority that her spirit returned to her body (Luke 8:55). The words were not some magic formula that anybody might use to raise the dead.

The girl not only came back to life, but was also healed of her sickness, for she was able to get out of bed and walk around. Always the loving Physician, Jesus instructed the astounded parents to give her some food lest she have a relapse. Divine miracles never replace common sense human care, otherwise we are tempting God.

As with previous miracles, Jesus told the witnesses to keep quiet (Mark 1:44; 3:12). Perhaps the word got out from the mourners that the girl had been "in a coma" and had not actually been dead. According to them, there had not been a miracle after all! However, there had been witnesses to the miracle. The law required only two or three witnesses for confirmation of truth (Deut. 17:6; 19:15), but for this miracle there were *five* witnesses! We have reason to conclude that Jairus and his wife became believers in Jesus Christ, though there is no further mention of them in the gospel record. All her life, the daughter was a witness to the power of Jesus Christ.

Yes, God's Servant is the conqueror over danger, demons, disease, and death. This series of miracles illustrates how Jesus met and helped all kinds of people, from His own disciples to a pair of demoniacs, and it assures us that He is able to help us today.

This does not mean that God *always* must rescue His people from danger (see Acts 12) or heal every affliction (see 2 Cor. 12:1–10), but it does mean that He holds the ultimate authority and that we need never fear. We are "more than conquerors through him that loved us" (Rom. 8:37).

QUESTIONS FOR PERSONAL REFLECTION
OR GROUP DISCUSSION

1. How can you explain the fact that the disciples saw Jesus do miracles and heard Him teach, yet were surprised that He could still the storm?

2. Why are we often amazed when we pray for something and God answers?

3. Discuss some reasons why difficult circumstances cause us to doubt God's care for us.

4. If we had an easy life, with no trials, do you think our faith would blossom more? What leads you to think that?

5. Wiersbe notes that Satan took away everything from the men controlled by demons: their jobs, their family, their friends. In what situations do you see Satan doing that today?

6. Discuss the courage and faith you think was involved for the sick woman to push through the crowd and believe Jesus could heal her. What was she risking?

7. If you had been Jairus, standing and waiting for Jesus to come and see about your daughter, how would witnessing this woman's healing have affected you?

8. What kind of faith did it take for Jairus to keep believing Jesus could make a difference even after he heard that his daughter was dead? Why?

9. As Jesus traveled through crowds of needy people, how do you think He decided whom to respond to?

10. For what do you need courage and faith?

Chapter Five

WILL ANYONE TRUST GOD'S SERVANT?

(Mark 6)

Charles Darwin said that *belief* was "the most complete of all distinctions between man and the lower animals." If this observation is true, it suggests that lack of faith on man's part puts him on the same level as the animals! Agnostic orator Col. Robert Ingersoll took a different point of view, for he once described a believer as "a songless bird in a cage." You would probably agree that his words better describe an *un*believer!

One of the central themes in this section of Mark's gospel is the unbelief of people who came into contact with God's Servant. All of these people had every reason to trust Jesus Christ, yet all of them failed to do so, including His own disciples! As you study this chapter, keep in mind the solemn admonition of Hebrews 3:12: "Take heed, brethren, lest there be in any of you an evil heart of unbelief, in departing from the living God." God takes unbelief seriously, and so should we.

THE UNBELIEF OF HIS ACQUAINTANCES (6:1–6)

Jesus returned to Nazareth, where a year before He had been rejected by the people and evicted from the synagogue (Luke 4:16–30). It was certainly an act of grace on His part to give the people another opportunity to hear His Word, believe, and be saved, and yet their hearts were still hard. This time, they did not evict Him: they simply did not take Him seriously.

Our Lord's reputation had once again preceded Him, so He was permitted to teach in the synagogue. Keep in mind that He was ministering to people who knew Him well, because Nazareth was His "hometown." However, these acquaintances had no spiritual perception at all. In fact, Jesus reminded them of what He had told them at that first dramatic visit, that a prophet is without honor in his own country and among his own people (Mark 6:4; Luke 4:24; John 4:44).

Two things astonished these people: His mighty works and His wonderful wisdom. Actually, Jesus did not do any mighty works while He was there, so the people must have been referring to the reports they had heard about His miracles (see Mark 1:28, 45; 3:7–8; 5:20–21). In fact, their unbelief hindered Jesus from having a greater ministry among them.

What was their problem? Why were they unable to trust Him and experience the wonders of His power and grace as had others? *They thought that they really knew Him.* After all, He had been their neighbor for nearly thirty years, they had seen Him at work in the carpenter's shop, and He appeared to be just another Nazarene. He was a "commoner," and the people saw no reason to commit themselves to Him!

"Familiarity breeds contempt" is a well-known maxim that goes all the way back to Publius the Syrian, who lived in 2 BC. Aesop wrote a fable to illustrate it. In Aesop's fable, a fox had never before seen a lion, and when he first met the king of the beasts, the fox was nearly frightened to death. At their second meeting, the fox was not frightened quite as much; and the third time he met the lion, the fox went up and chatted with him! "And so it is," Aesop concluded, "that familiarity makes even the most frightening things seem quite harmless."

The maxim, however, must be taken with a grain of salt. For example, can you imagine a loving husband and wife thinking less of each other because they know each other so well? Or two dear friends starting to despise each other because their friendship has deepened over the years? Phillips Brooks said it best: "Familiarity breeds contempt, only with contemptible things or among contemptible people." The contempt shown by the Nazarenes said nothing about Jesus Christ, but it said a great deal about them!

A tourist, eager to see everything in the art gallery, fled from picture to picture, scarcely noticing what was in the frames. "I didn't see anything very special here," he said to one of the guards as he left. "Sir," the guard replied, "it is not the pictures that are on trial here—it is the visitors."

A carpenter was a respected artisan in that day, but nobody expected a carpenter to do miracles or teach profound truths in the synagogue. Where did He get all this power and wisdom? From God or from Satan (see Mark 3:22)? And why did His brothers and sisters not possess this same power and wisdom? Even more, why did His brothers and sisters not believe in Him? The people who called Him "the son of Mary" were actually insulting Him, because in that day you identified a man by calling him the son of his father, not the son of his mother.

The people of Nazareth were "offended at him," which literally means "they stumbled over him." The Greek word gives us our English word *scandalize*. Kenneth Wuest wrote in his book *Wuest's Word Studies* (Eerdmans), "They could not explain Him, so they rejected Him." Jesus was certainly a "stone of stumbling" to them because of their unbelief (Isa. 8:14; Rom. 9:32–33; 1 Peter 2:8).

Twice in the gospel record you find Jesus marveling. As this passage reveals, He marveled at the unbelief of the Jews, and He marveled at the great faith of a Roman centurion, a Gentile (Luke 7:9). Instead of remaining at Nazareth, Jesus departed and made another circuit of the towns and villages in Galilee. His heart was broken as He saw the desperate plight of the people (Matt. 9:35–38), so He decided to send out His disciples to minister with His authority and power.

THE UNBELIEF OF HIS ENEMIES (6:7–29)

When the Lord originally called the twelve apostles, His purpose was to teach and train them so that they might assist Him and eventually be able to take His place when He returned to the Father (Mark 3:13–15). Before sending them out, He reaffirmed their authority to heal and to cast out demons (Mark 6:7), and He gave them some pointed instructions (see Matt. 10 for a more detailed account of this sermon).

He told them to take what they already owned and not go out and buy special equipment for their itinerant travels. They were not to be loaded down with extra baggage. (You cannot miss the note of urgency in this "commissioning sermon.") Jesus wanted them to be adequately supplied, but not to the point of ceasing to live by faith. The word *bag* means "a beggar's bag." They were definitely not to beg for either food or money.

As they ministered from place to place, they would encounter both hospitality and hostility, both friends and enemies. He cautioned them to stay at one house in each community and not to "pick and choose" when it came to their food and accommodations. After all, they were there to be profitable servants, not pampered guests. If a house or a village did not receive them, they had His permission to declare God's judgment on those people. It was customary for the Jews to shake the dust off their feet whenever they left Gentile territory, but for Jews to do this to their fellow Jews would be something new (Luke 10:10–11; Acts 13:51).

The word translated "send" in Mark 6:7 is *apostello* in the Greek and gives us our English word *apostle.* It means "to send someone with a special commission to represent another and to accomplish his work." Jesus gave these twelve men both the apostolic authority and the divine ability to do the job He sent them to do. They were not "on their own"; they represented Him in all that they did and said.

We noted before (Mark 3:16–19) that a comparison of the lists of the apostles' names reveals that the names are given in several pairs: Peter and Andrew, James and John, Philip and Bartholomew, etc. Jesus sent them out in pairs because it is always easier and safer for servants to travel and work together. "Two are better than one" (Eccl. 4:9), and the law, as previously observed, required two witnesses to verify a matter (Deut. 17:6; 19:15; 2 Cor. 13:1). They would not only help each other; they would also learn from each other.

The men went out and did what Jesus told them to do. It is remarkable that a band of ordinary men could go out in this way to represent Almighty God, and that they could demonstrate their authority by performing miracles. God's commandments always include His enablements (2 Cor. 3:5–6). They proclaimed the good news of the kingdom, called on sinners to repent, and healed many who were sick (Mark 6:12–13; Luke 9:6).

The reports of Christ's ministry, augmented by that of His disciples (Luke 9:7), even reached into the palace of Herod Antipas. Mark called him "King," which is what Herod wanted to be called, but in reality, godless Herod was only a tetrarch, the ruler of a fourth part of the nation. When Herod the Great died, the Romans divided his territory among his three sons, and Antipas was made tetrarch of Perea and Galilee.

Herod Antipas had married the daughter of King Aretas IV and then had divorced her so he could marry Herodias, the wife of his half-brother, Herod Philip. It was a wicked alliance that was contrary to the law of Moses (Lev. 18:16; 20:21), and the fearless John the Baptist had denounced the king for his sins. When Herod heard about the wonderful works of Jesus, he was sure that John the Baptist had come back from the dead to haunt him and condemn him! Herod's conscience was bothering him, but he was unwilling to face his sins honestly and repent.

At this point, Mark shifted into a flashback to explain how John the Baptist had been cruelly and unjustly arrested and slain. Even in this brief account, we sense the tension in the palace, for Herod feared John, privately listened to him preach, and was in a state of perplexity over what he should do. "Queen" Herodias, on the other hand, hated John, wanted to kill him, and patiently waited for the most convenient time. In their evil character and lawless deeds, these two remind us of Ahab and Jezebel (1 Kings 18—21).

The "strategic day" came (Mark 6:21 NASB) for Herodias to put her plan into action: the celebration of Herod's birthday. Royal feasts were extravagant both in their display of wealth and in their provision for pleasure. The Jews would not have permitted a woman to dance before a group of men, and most Gentile mothers would have forbidden a daughter to do what the daughter of Herodias did. (History informs us that the girl's name was Salome.) But the girl was a part of the mother's plan to get rid of John the Baptist, and Salome played her part well.

When Herod heard the girl's macabre request, he was "greatly distressed" (see Mark 14:34, where the same verb is used of Jesus), but he had to be true to his promise or lose face before a group of influential people. The word *oath* in Mark 6:26 is actually in the plural—"for his many oaths' sake"—because Herod had repeatedly declared his desire to reward the girl for her performance. This was one way he had of impressing his guests, but it backfired. Herod had not been courageous enough to obey John's word, but now he had to obey his own word! The result was the death of an innocent man.

It is remarkable that there is no evidence that any of the Jewish leaders did anything to rescue John the Baptist after he had been arrested. The common people considered John a prophet sent from God, but the religious leaders did not obey John's message (Mark 11:27–33). John's death was the first of three notable violent deaths in the history of Israel. The other two are the crucifixion of Christ and the stoning of Stephen (Acts 7). For the significance of these events, review the comments on Mark 3:22–30. Herod had feared that John's messages would stir up a revolt among the people, something he wanted to avoid. Also, he wanted to please his wife, even though it meant the murdering of a godly man.

John's disciples were permitted to take the body of their leader and bury it, and then they went to tell Jesus what had happened (Matt. 14:12). No doubt the report of John's death deeply stirred our Lord, for He knew that one day His own life would be laid down.

We meet Herod Antipas one more time in the Gospels, when he "tried" Jesus and hoped to see the Lord perform a miracle (Luke 23:6–12). Jesus would not even speak to this adulterer and murderer, let alone please him by doing a miracle! Jesus called Herod a "fox" (Luke 13:31–35), an apt description of this crafty man. In AD 39, Herod Agrippa (Acts 12:1), nephew of Herod Antipas, denounced his uncle to the Roman emperor, and Antipas was deposed and sent into exile. "For what shall it profit a man, if he shall gain the whole world, and lose his own soul?" (Mark 8:36).

THE UNBELIEF OF HIS DISCIPLES (6:30–56)

Jesus took His disciples to a secluded place so that they might rest after their labors. He wanted to discuss their ministry with them and prepare them for their next mission. As Vance Havner has said, "If you don't come apart and rest, you will come apart." Even God's Servant-Son needed time to rest, fellowship with His friends, and find renewal from the Father.

Another factor was the growing opposition of both the political and the religious leaders. Herod's murder of John the Baptist was evidence enough that the "climate" was now changing and that Jesus and His disciples had to be careful. In the next chapter, we shall encounter the hostility of the Jewish religious leaders, and, of course, the political enthusiasm of the crowds was always a problem (John 6:15ff.). The best thing to do was to get away.

But the overzealous crowds would not leave Him alone. They followed Him to the area near Bethsaida, hoping to see Him perform some miraculous cures (Luke 9:10–11; John 6:1ff.). In spite of the interruption to His plans, the Lord welcomed them, taught them the Word, and healed those who were afflicted. Having experienced interruptions many times in my own life and ministry, I marvel at His patience and grace! What an example for us to follow!

Mark recorded two miracles that Jesus performed.

(1) The feeding of the five thousand (vv. 33–44). Jesus sent the twelve apostles out to minister because He had compassion on the needy multitudes (Matt. 9:36–38). This time, the needy multitudes came to them—and the disciples wanted to send them away! As yet, they had not learned to look at life through the eyes of their Master. To them, the crowds were a problem, perhaps even a nuisance, but to Jesus, they were as sheep without a shepherd.

When D. L. Moody was building his great Sunday school in Chicago, children came to him from everywhere. They often passed by other churches and Sunday schools to be with Mr. Moody. When asked why he walked so far to attend Moody's Sunday school, one boy replied, "Because they love a fella over there!" The children could tell the difference.

The disciples had two suggestions for solving the problem: either send the people away to find their own food, or raise enough money to buy a bit of bread for everybody. As far as the disciples were concerned, they were in the wrong place at the wrong time, and nothing could be done! With that kind of approach, they would have made ideal committee members! Someone has defined a committee as a group of people who individually can do nothing and collectively decide that nothing can be done.

Jesus looked at the situation, not as a problem, but as an opportunity to trust the Father and glorify His name. An effective leader is someone who sees potential in problems and is willing to act by faith. Acting on the basis of human wisdom, His disciples saw the problem but not the potential. How many times God's people have complained, "If we only had enough money, we could do something!" Two hundred pence (denarii) would be the equivalent of a year's wages for the average laborer! The first step is not to measure *our* resources, but to determine God's will and trust Him to meet the need.

It was Andrew who found the lad with the lunch (John 6:8–9). The Lord had the people sit down in organized groups on the green grass (see Ps. 23:2; 78:19), quite a contrast to Herod's glittering sensual feast. Jesus took the little lunch, blessed it, broke it, and gave it to the disciples to distribute to the hungry people. The miracle took place in His hands, not in theirs, for whatever we give to Him, He can bless and multiply. We are not manufacturers; we are only distributors.

John tells us that Jesus used this miracle as the basis for a sermon on "the bread of life" (John 6:22ff.). After all, He did not perform miracles just to meet human needs, though that was important. He wanted each miracle to be a revelation of Himself, a sermon in action. For the most part, the people were amazed at the miracles, appreciated the help He gave them, but failed to get the spiritual message (John 12:37). They wanted the gift but not the Giver, the enjoyment of physical blessings but not the enrichment of spiritual blessings.

(2) The stilling of the storm (vv. 45–56). A number of miracles were involved in this event: Jesus walking on the water, Peter walking on the water (Mark did not record this; see Matt. 14:28–32), Jesus stilling the storm, and the boat arriving on shore the instant Jesus entered it (John 6:21). It was certainly a "night of wonders" for the Twelve!

Why did Jesus compel His disciples to leave? Because the crowd was getting restless, and there was danger they might start a popular uprising to make Jesus king (John 6:14–15). The Twelve were not ready to face this kind of test, because their ideas of the kingdom were still too national and political.

There was a second reason: He wanted to teach them a lesson on faith that would help prepare them for the work that lay ahead of them after He was gone. The disciples had just completed a very successful mission, healing the sick and preaching the gospel. They had shared in the miraculous feeding of five thousand people. They were on a "spiritual high," and this in itself was dangerous. It is good to be on the mountaintop if you don't get careless and step off a cliff.

Spiritual blessings must be balanced with burdens and battles, otherwise, we may become pampered children instead of mature sons and daughters. On a previous occasion, Jesus had led His disciples into a storm following an exciting day of teaching (Mark 4:35–41). Now, after a time of miraculous ministry, He again led them into a storm. In the book of Acts, it is interesting to note that the "storm" of official persecution began after the disciples had won five thousand people to Christ (Acts 4:1–4). Perhaps while they were in confinement, the apostles recalled the storm that followed the feeding of the five thousand, and they must have encouraged themselves with the assurance that Jesus would come to them and see them through.

Each new experience of testing demands of us more faith and courage. In that first storm experience, the disciples had Jesus in the boat with them, but this time, He was on the mountain praying for them. He was teaching them to live by faith. (For that matter, even when He was in the ship with them, they were still afraid!) The scene illustrates the situation of God's people today: We are in the midst of this stormy world, toiling and seemingly ready to sink, but He is in glory interceding for us. When the hour seems the darkest, He will come to us—and we will reach shore!

The waves that frightened the disciples (including the fishermen in the group) were only stairsteps to bring the Lord Jesus to them. He waited until their situation was so desperate that they could do nothing to help themselves. But why did He act as though He would pass them by? Because He wanted them to recognize Him, trust Him, and invite Him into the ship. They did not recognize Him, but instead screamed with fear because they thought He was a ghost!

Jesus reassured them with His word: "Take courage; it is I, do not be afraid" (Mark 6:50 NASB). At this point, Peter asked Jesus to let him walk on the water, but Mark omits this detail. Tradition says that Mark wrote as Peter's spokesman, so perhaps Peter was reticent to include this experience lest it give people the wrong impression. It is easy to criticize Peter for sinking—but have you ever gotten out of the boat yourself?

The disciples had failed their test because they lacked spiritual insight and receptive hearts. The miracle of the loaves and fishes had made no lasting impression on them. After all, if Jesus could multiply food and feed thousands of people, then surely He could protect them in the storm. Even a disciple of Jesus Christ can develop a hard heart if he fails to respond to the spiritual lessons that must be learned in the course of life and ministry.

As you review these two miracles, you see that Jesus Christ brings *provision* and *protection*. "The Lord is my shepherd; I shall not want.... I will fear no evil" (Ps. 23:1, 4). If we trust Him, we will always have sufficiency and security, no matter what the situation might be. The important thing is that we trust Him.

Mark closed this section on a positive note as he described the people who brought their sick for Jesus to heal. These people had faith and their faith was rewarded. This scene is in contrast to that in Nazareth, where very few were healed because the people lacked faith.

"And this is the victory that overcometh the world, even our faith" (1 John 5:4). Trust the Servant! He never fails.

QUESTIONS FOR PERSONAL REFLECTION
OR GROUP DISCUSSION

1. How do you define what it means to believe in something or someone?

2. From what you remember about Jesus' life, what would have convinced you that He was truly the Son of God?

3. What dynamics of a "hometown" would have made it difficult for the people of Nazareth to take Jesus seriously?

4. What today tempts us to take for granted that we know everything we need to know about Jesus?

5. What do you think would have been the greatest difficulty in being a disciple of Jesus?

6. What do you think would have been the greatest joy in being a disciple of Jesus?

7. To what contemporary evil or notorious character would you compare the wife of Herod who requested John the Baptist's head on a platter? Explain.

8. Make a list of what Jesus taught about God's nature when He fed the five thousand hungry people with only a small lunch.

9. What kinds of things did Jesus teach the disciples about God's nature when He walked across the water to their boat during a storm?

10. What does Peter's experience of walking on water teach you about faith that is relevant to your life currently?

Chapter Six

The Servant-Teacher

(Mark 7:1—8:26)

Throughout his gospel, Mark's emphasis is primarily on what Jesus did. However, in this section of our study you will find Mark recording some of the important *teachings* of the Lord. Mark also describes His ministry among the Gentiles, which would be of special interest to Roman readers. We see in this section three ministries of Jesus, the Servant-Teacher.

1. Teaching the Jews (7:1–23)

There are four stages in this drama, and the first is *accusation* (Mark 7:1–5). The Jewish religious leaders were now openly hostile toward the Lord and His ministry. It was not unusual for them to follow Him from place to place simply to watch for something to criticize. In this case, they accused the disciples of failing to practice the Jewish ceremonial washing. These washings had nothing to do with personal hygiene, nor were they commanded in the law. They were a part of the tradition that the scribes and Pharisees had given to the people to add to their burdens (Matt. 23:4).

Our Lord had already violated their Sabbath traditions (Mark 2:23—3:5), so the Jews were eager to accuse Him when they saw the disciples eat "with defiled hands." Why would such a seemingly trivial matter upset these religious leaders? Why would they feel compelled to defend their ceremonial washings? For one thing, these leaders resented it when our Lord openly flouted their authority. After all, these practices had been handed down from the fathers and carried with them the authority of the ages! The Jews called tradition "the fence of the law." It was not the law that protected the tradition, but the tradition that protected the law!

But something much more important was involved. Whenever the Jews practiced these washings, they declared that they were "special" and that other people were "unclean"! If a Jew went to the marketplace to buy food, he might be "defiled" by a Gentile or (God forbid!) a Samaritan. This tradition had begun centuries before to remind the Jews that they were God's elect people and therefore had to keep themselves separated. However, a good reminder had gradually degenerated into an empty ritual, and the result was pride and religious isolation.

These washings not only indicated a wrong attitude toward people, but they also conveyed a wrong idea of the nature of sin and personal holiness. Jesus made it clear in the Sermon on the Mount that true holiness is a matter of inward affection and attitude and not just outward actions and associations. The pious Pharisees thought they were holy because they obeyed the law and avoided external defilement. Jesus taught that a person who obeys the law externally can still break the law *in his heart,* and that external "defilement" has little connection with the condition of the inner person.

So the conflict was not only between God's truth and man's tradition, but also between two divergent views of sin and holiness. This confrontation was no incidental skirmish; it got to the very heart of true religious faith. Each new generation must engage in a similar conflict, for human nature is prone to hold on to worn-out man-made traditions and ignore or disobey the living Word of God. It is true that some traditions are helpful as reminders of our rich heritage, or as "cement" to bind generations, but we must constantly beware lest tradition take the place of truth. It does us good to examine our church traditions in the light of God's Word and to be courageous enough to make changes. (Note that the word *tradition* in 2 Thess. 2:15 refers to the body of doctrinal truth "handed down" from the apostles to leaders in the church. See also 2 Tim. 2:2.)

The next stage can be labeled *condemnation* (Mark 7:6–13) as Jesus defended His disciples and exposed the hypocrisy of their accusers. The first thing He did was to quote from the prophet Isaiah (Isa. 29:13), and then He brought in the law of Moses (Ex. 20:12; 21:17; Lev. 20:9). How could the Pharisees argue with the law and the prophets?

In defending their tradition, the Pharisees eroded their own characters and also the character of the Word of God. They were hypocrites, "playactors" whose religious worship was practiced in vain. True worship must come from the heart, and it must be directed by God's truth, not man's personal ideas. What a tragedy that religious people would ignorantly practice their religion and become the worse for doing it!

But they were not only destroying their character; they were also destroying the influence and authority of the very Word of God that they claimed to be defending. Note the tragic sequence: teaching their doctrines as God's Word (Mark 7:7); laying aside God's Word (Mark 7:8); rejecting God's Word (Mark 7:9); finally, robbing God's Word of its power (Mark 7:13). People who revere man-made traditions above the Word of God eventually lose the power of God's Word in their lives. No matter how devout they may appear, their hearts are far from God.

History reveals that the Jewish religious leaders came to honor their traditions far above the Word of God. Rabbi Eleazer said, "He who expounds the Scriptures in opposition to the tradition has no share in the world to come." The *Mishnah,* a collection of Jewish traditions in the *Talmud,* records, "It is a greater offense to teach anything contrary to the voice of the Rabbis than to contradict Scripture itself." But before we criticize our

Jewish friends, perhaps we should examine what influence "the church fathers" are having in our own Christian churches. We also may be guilty of replacing God's truth with man's traditions.

Once He had exposed their hypocrisy, Jesus then turned to the law of Moses and indicted them for breaking the fifth commandment. They had an ingenious way of breaking the law and not feeling guilty. Instead of using their wealth to support their parents, the Pharisees dedicated that wealth to God (*Corban* means "an offering, a gift") and claimed that the wealth could now be used only for "spiritual purposes." However, they continued to get the benefit of that wealth, even though it technically belonged to God. These men claimed to love God, but they had no love for their parents!

The third stage is *declaration* (Mark 7:14–16). Jesus announced to the whole crowd that the source of holy living is from within, not from without. Actually, He was declaring null and void the entire Mosaic system of "clean and unclean" foods, but at that time, He did not explain this radical truth to the crowd. Later, He did explain it in private to His own disciples.

But this declaration was surely understood by His enemies. They realized that He was breaking down one of the "walls" that separated the Jews from the Gentiles. Of course, the law itself was not set aside until Jesus died on the cross (Eph. 2:14–15; Col. 2:14), but the principle Jesus announced had been true throughout the ages. In every period of history, true holiness has always been a matter of the heart, a right relationship with God by faith. Ceremonial purity was a matter of external obedience to a law as evidence of that faith (Ps. 51:6, 10, 16–17). Moses made it clear in Deuteronomy that God wanted love and obedience to come from the heart, and not be merely outward obedience to rules (note Deut. 6:4–5; 10:12; 30:6, 20).

Our Lord's *explanation* (Mark 7:17–23) was given privately to His disciples when they asked Him "concerning the parable." His explanation seems obvious to us, but we must remember that these twelve men had been brought up under the strict Jewish dietary code that categorized all foods as either "clean" or "unclean" (Lev. 11). In fact, Acts 10:14 suggests that Peter kept a kosher household for years even after he had heard this truth. It is not easy to change our religious traditions.

The human heart is sinful and produces all manner of evil desires, thoughts, and actions, everything from murder to envy ("an evil eye"). Jesus had no illusions about human nature, as do some liberal theologians and humanistic teachers today. He realized that man is a sinner, unable to control or change his own nature, *and that is why Jesus came to earth—to die for lost sinners.*

The Jewish dietary laws were given by God to teach His chosen people to make a difference between what was clean and what was unclean. (No doubt there were also some practical reasons involved, such as sanitation and health.) To disobey these laws was a matter of ceremonial defilement, and that was an external matter. Food *ends up* in the stomach, but sin *begins* in the heart. The food we eat is digested and the waste evacuated, but sin remains and it produces defilement and death.

This dramatic lesson on "truth vs. tradition" could only irritate the Jewish religious leaders more and make them want to silence Jesus. This increased opposition was the reason He departed from the crowded places and took His disciples into Gentile territory.

Before we leave this section, however, it might be good for us to contrast man's traditions and God's truth.

Man's traditions	God's truth
Outward forms—bondage	Inward faith—liberty
Trifling rules	Fundamental principles
Outward piety	True inward holiness
Neglect, replace the Word	Exalts the Word of God

2. HELPING THE GENTILES (7:24—8:9)

Mark records three miracles that Jesus performed as He ministered to the Gentiles in the region of Tyre and Sidon. This is the only recorded instance of our Lord actually leaving Palestine. He was practicing what He had just taught the disciples: There is no difference between Jews and Gentiles, for all are sinners and need the Savior.

(1) **Casting out a demon (7:24–30).** Of the thirty-five recorded miracles in the Gospels, four directly involve women: the healing of Peter's mother-in-law (Mark 1:30–31); the raising of the widow's son (Luke 7:11–17); the raising of Lazarus (John 11); and the casting out of the demon as recorded here.

Jesus came to this area (about forty miles from Capernaum) so that He might have some privacy, but a concerned mother discovered He was there and came to Him for help. There were many obstacles in her way, yet she overcame them all by faith and got what she needed.

To begin with, her nationality was against her: She was a Gentile and Jesus was a Jew. Besides that, she was a woman, and society in that day was dominated by men. Satan was against her, for one of his demons had taken control in her daughter's life. The disciples were against her; they wanted Jesus to send her away and let Him (and them) have some rest. For a time, it looked as though even Jesus was against her! It was not an easy situation, and yet she triumphed because of her great faith.

Samuel Rutherford, the saintly Scottish minister who suffered greatly for Christ, once wrote to a friend: "It is faith's work to claim and challenge loving-kindnesses out of all the roughest strokes of God." That is exactly what this Gentile mother did, and we today have much that we can learn from her about faith.

When she first asked Him for help, Jesus did not even answer her! Encouraged by His silence, the disciples urged Him to send her away. When Jesus did speak, it was not to the woman but to the disciples, and

His words seem to exclude her completely: "I am not sent but unto the lost sheep of the house of Israel" (Matt. 15:24). However, none of these barriers stopped her from pressing on with her plea.

The first time she cried for help, the mother addressed Jesus as "Son of David," a Jewish title, but the next time she cried out for help, she simply said, "Lord, help me" (Matt. 15:25). It was then that Jesus spoke about feeding the children (Israel) first and not throwing their food to "the little pet puppies." Jesus was not calling the Gentiles "dirty scavenger dogs" as did many of the proud Jews; He was giving her hope, and she took hold of it.

Her reply revealed that faith had triumphed. She did not deny the special place of the "children" (Jews) in God's plan, nor did she want to usurp it. All she wanted were a few crumbs of blessing from the table, for, after all, "Salvation is of the Jews" (John 4:22). His heart must have rejoiced when she took *His very words* and used them as a basis for her plea! She accepted her place, she believed His Word, and she persisted in her plea, and Jesus not only met her need, but commended her for her faith.

It is significant that the two times in the gospel record when Jesus commended "great faith," He was responding to the faith of Gentiles and not Jews: this Syrophoenician woman and the Roman centurion (Matt. 8:5–13). It is also worth noting that in both situations, Jesus healed *at a distance,* suggesting the spiritual distance between Jews and Gentiles at that time (Eph. 2:11–22). Finally, the people of Tyre and Sidon were not known for their faith (Matt. 11:21–22), yet this woman dared to believe that Jesus could deliver her daughter.

Great faith is faith that takes God at His Word and will not let go until God meets the need. Great faith can lay hold of even the slightest encouragement and turn it into a fulfilled promise. "Lord, increase our faith."

(2) Healing a deaf man (7:31–37). The region of Decapolis ("ten cities") was also Gentile territory, but before Jesus left the region, the people were glorifying the God of Israel (Matt. 15:30–31). The man they brought to Jesus was handicapped both by deafness and an impediment in his speech, and Jesus healed him. This miracle is recorded only by Mark and would be especially appreciated by his Roman readers, since the "ten cities" region was like a "Rome away from Rome."

Jesus took the man away from the crowd so that the healing would be private and the man would not become a public attraction. Since the man was deaf, he could not hear our Lord's words, but he could feel Jesus' fingers in his ear and the touch on his tongue, and this would encourage the man's faith. The "sigh" was an inward groan, our Lord's compassionate response to the pain and sorrow sin has brought into the world. It was also a prayer to the Father on behalf of the handicapped man. (The same word is used in connection with prayer in Rom. 8:23, and the noun in Rom. 8:26.)

Ephphatha is an Aramaic word that means "be opened, be released." The man did not hear Jesus speak, but the creation heard the command of the Creator, and the man was healed. Both the tongue and the ears functioned normally again. In spite of our Lord's strict command for the people to keep quiet about the miracles, they told the news everywhere (see Mark 1:34, 44; 3:12; 5:43), and this resulted in a large crowd gathering and bringing people who were ill or handicapped. Even though Jesus was trying to enjoy some rest, He took time to heal them all. The result? These Gentiles "glorified the God of Israel" (Matt. 15:31).

(3) Feeding the four thousand (8:1–9). Those who try to find contradictions in the Bible often confuse this miracle with the feeding of the five thousand, which is recorded in all four gospels. Only Matthew and Mark record this event, and it is not difficult to distinguish it from the other miracle of the multiplying of bread and fish. The first miracle took place in Galilee, near Bethsaida, and involved predominantly Jews. This miracle took place near the Decapolis and involved mostly Gentiles. In the first miracle, Jesus started with five loaves and two fish, while here He had seven loaves "and a few fish." The five thousand had been with Him one day, but the four thousand had been with him three days. Twelve baskets of fragments were left over after the five thousand were fed, but only seven baskets after the four thousand were fed. There were even two different kinds of baskets used: for the five thousand, small wicker lunch baskets *(kophinos);* for the four thousand, large hampers, big enough to hold a man *(spuris,* see Acts 9:25).

Once again, we are encouraged by our Lord's compassion and His complete control over the situation. However, we are discouraged by the blindness and unbelief of the disciples. Had they completely forgotten the previous miracle? Let's not be too hard on them. How many times have *we* forgotten the mercies of the Lord? We need to remind ourselves that Jesus Christ is still the same and has the solution to every problem. All we need do is trust Him, give Him our all, and obey.

3. WARNING THE DISCIPLES (8:10–26)

Jesus and the disciples crossed to the western side of the Sea of Galilee where they were met by the Pharisees who were still angry at Him because of His earlier indictment of their hypocrisy (Mark 7:1–23). This time they tempted Him to prove His divine authority by giving them a sign from heaven. They did not want an earthly miracle, such as the healing of a sick person. They wanted Him to do something spectacular, like bring fire from heaven or bread from heaven (John 6:30–31). This would prove He was indeed sent from God.

Our Lord's response was one of deep grief and disappointment (see Mark 7:34). How tragic that the religious leaders of God's chosen people should be so hardhearted and spiritually blind! Their desire for a sign from heaven was but another evidence of their unbelief, for faith does not ask for signs. True faith takes God at His Word and is satisfied with the inward witness of the Spirit.

Since Mark was writing primarily for Gentile readers, he did not include our Lord's words concerning the sign of the prophet Jonah (Matt. 16:4; and see Matt. 12:38–41). What is "the sign of Jonah"? Death, burial, and resurrection. The proof that Jesus is what He claimed to be is the fact of His own death, burial, and resurrection (Acts 2:22–36; 3:12–26).

Jesus left them and crossed to the east side of the Sea of Galilee, and en route taught His disciples an important spiritual lesson. It appears that they were almost as blind as the Pharisees! The men were having a private discussion about their food supply, because somebody had forgotten to pack bread. Who was to blame?

It must have grieved Jesus that His hand-picked helpers were so spiritually obtuse. The fact that He had multiplied bread on two occasions and fed over ten thousand people had apparently made little impression on them! Why worry and argue over one loaf of bread when you have Jesus in the boat with you? Their minds were dull, their hearts were hard (see Mark 6:52), their eyes were blind, and their ears were deaf (see Mark 4:11–12).

God's people often have a tendency to forget His blessings (Ps. 103:1–2). He meets our needs, but then when the next problem arises, we complain or become frightened. As long as we are with Him, we can be sure He will care for us. It would do us all good to pause occasionally and remind ourselves of His goodness and faithfulness.

But the main lesson had to do with *leaven* (yeast) and not with bread. In the Bible, leaven is consistently a symbol of evil. Each Passover season, the Jews had to remove all leaven from their dwellings (Ex. 12:18–20), and leaven was not allowed with the offerings (Ex. 23:18; 34:25; Lev. 2:11; 6:17). Evil, like leaven, is small and hidden, but it spreads and soon infects the whole (Gal. 5:9).

The Bible uses leaven as a picture of false doctrine (Gal. 5:1–9), unjudged sin in the church (1 Cor. 5), and hypocrisy (Luke 12:1). In this context, Jesus warned them about the teaching (false doctrine) of the Pharisees and the followers of Herod. The Pharisees "said but they did not"; in other words, they practiced and encouraged hypocrisy (note Mark 7:6). The Herodians were a worldly group who catered to Herod, accepted the Roman way of life, and saw in Herod and his rule the promised kingdom for the Jewish nation. If this false teaching got into the hearts and minds of the disciples, it would infect them and pollute the truth Jesus had given them to proclaim about Himself and His kingdom.

We can never be too careful about detecting and avoiding false doctrine. Only a small deviation from the Word may get into an individual or a church, but before long it will grow and infect everything. Our Lord did not often say "Beware!" but when He did, it was important!

In this section, Mark recorded two miracles that are not found in the other Gospels: (1) the healing of the deaf man who had a speech impediment (Mark 7:31–37), and (2) the healing of the blind man outside Bethsaida (Mark 8:22–26). Perhaps we can see in these two men illustrations of the disciples' spiritual condition described in Mark 8:18! Jewish readers would connect these two miracles with the messianic promises in Isaiah 35.

In both these situations, friends brought the men to Jesus, and in both situations, Jesus led the men away from the crowds. In fact, in the latter case, He took the man *outside the city*. Why? Probably because the city of Bethsaida had already been judged because of its unbelief (Matt. 11:21–24). No more evidence would be given to them.

The unique thing about this miracle of healing is that it occurred *gradually* and not instantly. The Gospels record the healing of at least seven blind men, and they show that our Lord used a variety of approaches. Perhaps it was the atmosphere of unbelief in Bethsaida that hindered Him (see Mark 6:5–6), or it may have been the spiritual condition of the man himself. For some reason not given, the man was not ready for instant sight, so Jesus restored him gradually. The fact that the man recognized men and trees suggests that he had not been born blind but had been blinded by accident or disease.

The man was not from Bethsaida, for Jesus sent him home and cautioned him not to enter that town. Now that he had been healed, why go to unbelieving Bethsaida where Jesus had been rejected? His job was to go home and spread the good news of the kingdom, and to demonstrate its power by showing others what Jesus had done for him (see Mark 2:11; 5:34; 10:52). Should he not give another opportunity to the people in Bethsaida? Perhaps they would believe if they heard how Jesus had restored his sight. No, Bethsaida had been given adequate evidence, but still had refused to believe. It is a dangerous thing for anybody to reject the message of God and harden his or her heart in unbelief.

The disciples learned some valuable lessons on this trip, lessons that they would need to remember and apply in later years of ministry. We today need to learn these same lessons: (1) don't seek after signs, but live by faith in His Word; (2) trust Jesus to meet needs; (3) avoid the leaven of false doctrine; (4) let Jesus work as He wills, and expect variety in His working.

Mark recorded the events of some busy days in the ministry of God's Servant! Next he will take us "behind the scenes" as the Servant instructs His disciples and prepares them for His death on the cross.

QUESTIONS FOR PERSONAL REFLECTION
OR GROUP DISCUSSION

1. Jesus' servanthood stood in sharp contrast to the habits of the religious leaders of His day, who used their positions to gain power over the people. In what ways do we see that same problem today?

2. On a scale of 1–10 (1=extremely easy, 10=extremely difficult), how easy do you think it is to obey God outwardly through ceremony and yet be disobedient in your heart attitude? What spiritual problem does this create?

3. What are the positive effects of longtime traditions?

4. What are the negative effects of longtime traditions?

5. What hypocrisies do you see around you that Jesus would have rebuked?

6. Do you think God's truth conflicts in any ways with the traditions in the church you belong to? If so, in what ways?

7. Wiersbe says, "Great faith is faith that takes God at His Word and will not let go until God meets the need." Describe an act of great faith that you have seen or heard about or experienced.

8. Through His miracles Jesus helped people solve the problems they faced. What does this teach us about how Jesus can help us face our own problems?

9. Even though the disciples witnessed Jesus' miracles, they were still afraid when they faced trials. If God has come through for us in our lives, why do we still worry when problems arise?

10. What is the Servant-Teacher asking you to take to heart in your current circumstances?

Chapter Seven

THE SERVANT'S SECRETS

(Mark 8:27—9:50)

A secret has been defined as "something you tell one person at a
time." From time to time, Jesus shared special "secrets" with His
disciples, and three of them are given here. Believers today need
to understand and apply these spiritual secrets if their own lives are to be
all that God wants them to be.

1. SUFFERING LEADS TO GLORY (8:27—9:13)

Jesus had been preparing His disciples for this private meeting at which
He intended to reveal to them what would happen to Him at Jerusalem.
He had given hints along the way, but now He would explain matters to
them more fully. For the site, He selected Caesarea Philippi, a town about
twenty-five miles north of Bethsaida, sitting at the foot of beautiful Mount
Hermon. The town was named after Augustus Caesar and Herod Philip,
and it contained a marble temple dedicated to Augustus. It was a place
dedicated to the glory of Rome, and that glory is now gone, but the glory
of Jesus Christ remains and will go on eternally.

Confession (8:27–30). If you were to go around asking your friends,
"What do people say about me?" they would take it as an evidence of
pride. What difference does it really make what people think or say about
us? We are not that important! But what people believe and say about

Jesus Christ *is* important, for He is the Son of God and the only Savior of sinners.

Your confession concerning Jesus Christ is a matter of life or death (John 8:21, 24; 1 John 2:22–27; 4:1–3). The citizens of Caesarea Philippi would say, "Caesar is lord!" That confession might identify them as loyal Roman citizens, but it could never save them from their sins and from eternal hell. The only confession that saves us is "Jesus is Lord!" (1 Cor. 12:1–3) when it comes from a heart that truly believes in Him (Rom. 10:9–10).

It is remarkable the number of different opinions the people held about Jesus, though the same situation probably exists today. That some thought He was John the Baptist is especially perplexing, since John and Jesus had been seen publicly together. They were quite different in personality and ministry (Matt. 11:16–19), so it seems strange that the people would confuse them.

John the Baptist came "in the spirit and power of Elijah" (Luke 1:17), in a ministry of judgment, whereas Jesus came in a spirit of meekness and service. John performed no miracles (John 10:41), but Jesus was a miracle-worker. John even dressed like the prophet Elijah (2 Kings 1:8; Mark 1:6). How could the people confuse the two?

Some said that Jesus was one of the prophets, perhaps Jeremiah (Matt. 16:14). Jeremiah was "the weeping prophet," and Jesus was a Man of Sorrows, so there is a definite parallel. Jeremiah called the people to true repentance from the heart, and so did Jesus. Both men were misunderstood and rejected by their own people, both condemned the false religious leaders and the hypocritical worship in the temple, and both were persecuted by those in authority.

In His words and His works, Jesus gave every evidence to the people that He was the Son of God, the Messiah, and yet they did not get the message. Instead of diligently seeking for the truth, the people listened to popular opinion and followed it, just as many people do today. They had opinions instead of convictions, and this is what led them astray. Elbert Hubbard defined public opinion as "the judgment of the incapable many, opposed to that of the discerning few." Thank God for the discerning few!

Peter's confession was bold and uncompromising, just as ours should be: "Thou art the Christ, the Son of the living God" (Matt. 16:16). The word *Christ* means "the Anointed One, the promised Messiah." Prophets, priests, and kings were all anointed when installed in their offices, and our Lord holds all three offices.

Why did Jesus warn them to keep quiet about Him? For one thing, the disciples themselves still had much to learn about Him and what it truly meant to follow Him. The religious leaders of the nation had already made up their minds about Him, and to proclaim Him as Messiah now would only upset God's plans. The common people wanted to see His miracles, but they had little desire to submit to His message. To announce Him as Messiah might well result in a political uprising that would only do harm.

Confusion (8:31–38). Now that they had confessed their faith in Christ (but see John 6:66–71), the disciples were ready for the "secret" Jesus wanted to share with them: He was going with them to Jerusalem, where He would die on a cross. From this point on, Mark will focus on their journey to Jerusalem, and the emphasis will be on Jesus' approaching death and resurrection (Mark 9:30–32; 10:32–34).

This announcement stunned the disciples. If He is indeed the Christ of God, as they had confessed, then why would He be rejected by the religious leaders? Why would these leaders crucify Him? Did not the Old Testament Scriptures promise that the Messiah would defeat all their enemies and establish a glorious kingdom for Israel? There was something wrong somewhere and the disciples were confused.

True to character, it was Peter who expressed their concern. One minute Peter was led by God to confess his faith in Jesus Christ (Matt. 16:17), and the next minute he was thinking like an unbelieving man and expressing the thoughts of Satan! This is a warning to us that when we argue with God's Word, we open the door for Satan's lies. Peter began rebuking his Master, and Mark used the same word that describes our Lord's rebuking of the demons (Mark 1:25; 3:12).

Peter's protest was born out of his ignorance of God's will and his deep love for his Lord. One minute Peter was a "rock," and the next minute he was a stumbling block! Dr. G. Campbell Morgan said, "The man who loves Jesus, but who shuns God's method, is a stumbling block to Him." Peter did not yet understand the relationship between suffering and glory. He would eventually learn this lesson and would even emphasize it in his first epistle (note 1 Peter 1:6–8; 4:13—5:10).

Note, however, that when Jesus rebuked Peter, He also "looked on his disciples," because they agreed with Peter's assessment of the situation! Steeped in Jewish traditional interpretation, they were unable to understand how their Messiah could ever suffer and die. To be sure, some of the prophets had written about the Messiah's sufferings, but much more had been written about the Messiah's glory. Some rabbis even taught that there would be *two* Messiahs, one who would suffer and one who would reign (see 1 Peter 1:10–12). No wonder the disciples were confused.

But the problem was more than theological; it was very practical. Jesus had called these men to follow Him, and they knew that whatever happened to Him would happen to them. If there was a cross in *His* future, there would be one in *their* future as well. That would be reason enough to disagree with Him! In spite of their devotion to Him, the disciples were still ignorant of the true relationship between the cross and the crown. They were following Satan's philosophy (glory without suffering) instead of God's philosophy (suffering transformed into glory). Which philosophy you accept will determine how you live and how you serve.

Mark 8:34 indicates that, though Jesus and His disciples had met in private, the crowds were not far away. Jesus summoned the people and taught them what He taught His own disciples: *There is a price to pay for true discipleship.* He knew that the crowds were following Him only because of the miracles, and that most of the people were unwilling to pay the price to become true disciples.

Jesus laid down three conditions for true discipleship: (1) we must surrender ourselves completely to Him; (2) we must identify with Him in suffering and death; and (3) we must follow Him obediently, wherever He leads. If we live for ourselves, we will lose ourselves, but if we lose ourselves for His sake and the gospel's, we will find ourselves.

Denying self is not the same as self-denial. We practice self-denial when, for a good purpose, we occasionally give up things or activities. But we deny self when we surrender ourselves to Christ and determine to obey His will. This once-for-all dedication is followed by a daily "dying to self" as we take up the cross and follow Him. From the human point of view, we are losing ourselves, but from the divine perspective, we are finding ourselves. When we live for Christ, we become more like Him, and this brings out our own unique individuality.

But note the motivation for true discipleship: "for my sake and the gospel's" (Mark 8:35). To lose yourself is not an act of desperation; it is an act of devotion. But we do not stop there: Personal devotion should lead to practical duty, the sharing of the gospel with a lost world. "For my sake" could lead to selfish religious isolationism, so it must be balanced with "and the gospel's." Because we live for Him, we live for others.

Discipleship is a matter of profit and loss, a question of whether we will *waste* our lives or *invest* our lives. Note the severe warning Jesus gives us here: Once we have spent our lives, we cannot buy them back! Remember, He was instructing His *disciples,* men who had already confessed Him as the Son of God. He was not telling them how to be saved and go to heaven, but how to save their lives and make the most of their opportunities on earth. "Losing your soul" is the equivalent of wasting your life, missing the great opportunities God gives you to make your life count. You may "gain the whole world" and be a success in the eyes of men, and yet have nothing to show for your life when you stand before God. If that happens, though you may own the whole world, it would not be a sufficient price to give to God to buy another chance at life.

Is there any reward for the person who is a true disciple? Yes, there is: He becomes more like Jesus Christ and one day shares in His glory. Satan promises you glory, but in the end, you receive suffering. God promises you suffering, but in the end, that suffering is transformed into glory. If we acknowledge Christ and live for Him, He will one day acknowledge us and share His glory with us.

Confirmation (9:1–8). It takes faith to accept and practice this lesson on discipleship, so six days later the Lord gave a dazzling proof that God indeed does transform suffering into glory. (Luke's "about eight days" is inclusive of the day of the lesson and the day of the glory, Luke 9:28.) He took Peter, James, and John to the top of a mountain (it may have been Mount Hermon), and there He revealed His glory. This event was a vivid confirmation of His words as recorded in Mark 8:38, as well as a demonstration of the glory of the future kingdom (Mark 9:1; John 1:14; 2 Peter 1:12–21). The message was clear: first the suffering, then the glory.

Moses represented the law and Elijah the prophets, both of which find their fulfillment in Jesus Christ (Luke 24:25–27; Heb. 1:1–2). Moses had died and his body was buried, but Elijah had been raptured to heaven (2 Kings 2:11). When Jesus returns, He will raise the bodies of the saints who died and will rapture the living saints (1 Thess. 4:13–18). Jesus will one day establish His glorious kingdom and fulfill the many promises made through the prophets. Christ's sufferings and death would not *prevent* God from establishing His kingdom; rather, by solving the sin problem in God's world, the cross would help to make the kingdom possible.

The word *transfigured* describes a change on the outside that comes from the inside. It is the opposite of "masquerade," which is an outward change that does not come from within. Jesus allowed His glory to radiate through His whole being, and the mountaintop became a Holy of Holies! As you meditate on this event, keep in mind that He has shared this glory with us and promised us a glorious home forever (John 17:22–24). According to Romans 12:1–2 and 2 Corinthians 3:18, believers today can experience this same transfiguration glory.

The three disciples had gone to sleep while Jesus was praying (Luke 9:29, 32), a failure they would repeat in the garden of Gethsemane (Mark 14:32–42). They almost missed seeing Moses and Elijah and Jesus in His glory! Peter's suggestion reflects again human thinking and not divine wisdom. How wonderful it would be to stay on the mountaintop and bask in His glory! But discipleship means denying self, taking up a cross, and following Him, and you cannot do that and selfishly stay on the mount of glory. There are needs to be met in the valley below. If we want to share the glory of Christ on the mountaintop, we must be willing to follow Him into the sufferings of the valley below.

The Father interrupted Peter's speech and focused their attention, not on the vision, but on the Word of God: "Hear him!" The memory of visions will fade, but the unchanging Word abides forever. The glorious vision was not an end in itself; it was God's way of confirming the Word (see 2 Peter 1:12–21). Discipleship is not built on spectacular visions but on the inspired, unchanging Word of God. Nor do we put Moses, Elijah, and Jesus on the same level, as Peter hinted. It is "Jesus only"—His Word, His will, His kingdom, and His glory.

The three men were not allowed to tell the other nine what they had seen on the mount. No doubt their explanation after His resurrection brought great encouragement to the believers who themselves would experience suffering and death for His sake.

Correction (9:11–13). The disciples now understood God's plan much better, but they were still confused about the coming of Elijah to prepare the way for the Messiah. They knew the prophecies in Malachi 3:1 and 4:5–6, and that their teachers expected these prophecies to be fulfilled before the Messiah appeared (John 1:21). Had Elijah already come and they missed him, or was he yet to come? Perhaps the appearing of Elijah on the mount was the fulfillment of the prophecy.

Jesus made two facts clear. First, for those who had trusted in Him, this "Elijah" was John the Baptist, for John had indeed prepared the way before Him. John had denied that he was Elijah come from the dead (John 1:21, 25), but he did minister in the "spirit and power of Elijah" (Luke 1:16–17). Second, there would be a future coming of Elijah, just as Malachi had predicted (Matt. 17:11), before the time of great tribulation. Some students connect this with Revelation 11:2–12. The nation did not accept John's ministry. Had they received John, he would have served as the "Elijah" God sent, and they also would have received Jesus. Instead, they rejected both men and allowed them to be slain.

2. POWER COMES FROM FAITH (9:14–29)

The Christian life is "a land of hills and valleys" (Deut. 11:11). In one day, a disciple can move from the glory of heaven to the attacks of hell. When our Lord and His three friends returned to the other nine disciples, they found them involved in a dual problem: They were unable to deliver a boy from demonic control, and the scribes were debating with them and perhaps even taunting them because of their failure. As always, it was Jesus who stepped in to solve the problem.

The boy was both deaf and mute (Mark 9:17, 25), and the demon was doing his best to destroy him. Imagine what it would be like for that father to try to care for the boy and protect him! Jesus had given His disciples authority to cast out demons (Mark 6:7, 13), and yet their ministry to the boy was ineffective. No wonder the Lord was grieved with them! How often He must be grieved with us when we fail to use the spiritual resources He has graciously given to His people!

Since the disciples had failed, the desperate father was not even sure that Jesus could succeed; hence his statement, "If you can do anything" (Mark 9:22 NASB). However, the father was honest enough to admit his own unbelief and to ask the Lord to help him and his son. Jesus did cast out the demon and restore the boy to his father.

The main lesson of this miracle is the power of faith to overcome the enemy (Mark 9:19, 23–24; and see Matt. 17:20). Why had the nine disciples failed? Because they had been careless in their personal spiritual walk and had neglected prayer and fasting (Mark 9:29). The authority that Jesus had given them was effective only if exercised by faith, but faith must be cultivated through spiritual discipline and devotion. It may be that the absence of their Lord, or His taking the three disciples with Him and leaving them behind, had dampened their spiritual fervor and diminished their faith. Not only did their failure embarrass them, but it also robbed the Lord of glory and gave the enemy opportunity to criticize. It is our faith in Him that glorifies God (Rom. 4:20).

3. SERVICE LEADS TO HONOR (9:30–50)

Jesus was still leading His disciples to Jerusalem, and as they went, He reminded them of what would happen to Him there. Note that He also reminded them of His resurrection, but they were unable to understand what He was saying (see Matt. 17:9). They were "exceedingly sorry" ("deeply grieved," Matt. 17:23 NASB).

However, they were not grieved enough to set aside their personal dispute over which of them was the greatest! After they heard what Jesus had said about His own suffering and death, you would think they would have forgotten their own selfish plans and concentrated on Him. Perhaps the fact that Peter, James, and John had gone on the mount with Jesus had added some fuel to the fires of competition.

To teach them (and us) a lesson on honor, Jesus set a child before them and explained that the way to be first is to be last, and the way to be last is to be the servant of all. The unspoiled child is an example of submission and humility. A child knows he is a child and acts like a child, and that is his secret of attracting love and care. The child who tries to impress us by acting like an adult does not get the same attention.

True humility means knowing yourself, accepting yourself, being yourself—your *best* self—and giving of yourself for others. The world's philosophy is that you are "great" if others are working for you, but Christ's message is that greatness comes from our serving others. Since the words *child* and *servant* are the same in the Aramaic language, it is easy to see why Jesus connected the two. If we have the heart of a child, we will have little difficulty being servants, and if we have the attitude of servants, we will welcome the children as the representatives of Jesus Christ and the Father.

At this point, John felt it necessary to defend the disciples (Mark 9:38–41) by pointing out their zeal. Imagine telling a man to stop casting out demons when the nine disciples had failed to deliver the deaf and mute boy from Satan's power! To use the name of Jesus is the same as working under His authority, so the men had no right to stop the man. "To his own master he standeth or falleth" (Rom. 14:4).

Mark 9:40 should be compared with Matthew 12:30: "He that is not with me is against me." Both statements declare the impossibility of neutrality when it comes to our relationship with Jesus Christ. Since we cannot be neutral, if we are not for Him, we must be against Him; if we are not against Him, we must be for Him. The anonymous exorcist was bringing glory to His name, so he had to be *for* the Savior and not against Him.

But it is not necessary to perform great miracles to prove our love for Christ. When we lovingly receive a child or compassionately share a cup of cold water, we are giving evidence that we have the humble heart of a servant. After all, we are serving Christ, and that is the highest service in the world (Matt. 25:31–46).

Jesus did not treat John's statement lightly; in fact, He went on to explain the danger of causing others to stumble and therefore stop serving the Lord (Mark 9:42–50). "These little ones" refers to all God's children who follow Christ and seek to serve Him. The way believers treat others in the family of God is a serious thing, and God wants us to "have peace one with another" (Mark 9:50). The disciples did not get along with each other, nor did they get along with other believers!

This solemn message about hell carries a warning to all of us to deal drastically with sin. Whatever in our lives makes us stumble, and therefore causes others to stumble, must be removed as if by surgery. The hand, foot, and eye would be considered valuable parts of the body, yet they must be removed if they are causing sin. Of course, the Lord is not commanding literal physical surgery, since He had already made it clear that sin comes from the heart (Mark 7:20–23). What He is teaching is that sin is to the inner person what a cancerous tumor is to the body, and it must be dealt with drastically.

Some people are shocked to hear from the lips of Jesus such frightening words about hell (see Isa. 66:24). Jesus believed in a place called hell, a place of eternal torment and righteous punishment (see Luke 16:19ff.). After an army chaplain told his men that he did not believe in hell, some of them suggested that his services were not needed. After all, if there is no hell, then why worry about death? But if there is a hell, then the chaplain was leading them astray! Either way, they would be better off without him!

The word translated "hell" is *gehenna*. It comes from a Hebrew phrase "the valley *[ge]* of Hinnon," referring to an actual valley outside Jerusalem where wicked King Ahaz worshipped Molech, the fire god, and even sacrificed his children in the fire (2 Chron. 28:1–3; Jer. 7:31; 32:35).

Some manuscripts do not have Isaiah 66:24 quoted in Mark 9:44 and 46, but the statement is quoted in verse 48, and that one verse is sufficient. Hell is not temporary; it is forever (see Rev. 20:10). How essential it is for sinners to trust Jesus Christ and be delivered from eternal hell, and how important it is for believers to get the message out to a lost world!

"But isn't that too great a sacrifice to ask from us?" someone might argue. "To deal that drastically with sin would cost us too much!" In Mark 9:49–50, Jesus used the concept of "living sacrifices" to illustrate His point (see Rom. 12:1–2). The sacrifice ends up on the altar and is consumed by the fire. Would you rather endure the fires of hell as a lost sinner or the purifying fires of God as a sacrifice for His glory? Remember, Satan promises you glory now, but the pain comes later. Jesus calls us to suffering now, and then we will enjoy the glory.

The Jews were not allowed to put leaven or honey on their sacrifices, but they were required to use salt (Lev. 2:11, 13). Salt speaks of purity and preservation. It was used in Old Testament days in the establishing of covenants. The disciples were God's salt (Matt. 5:13), but they were in danger of losing their flavor and becoming worthless. Our salt today is purified and does not lose its taste, but the salt of that day contained impurities and could lose its flavor. Once you have lost that precious Christian character, how will you restore it?

Instead of rebuking others, the disciples should have been examining their own hearts! It is easy to lose our "saltiness" and become useless to God. Christians will experience the fire of trials and persecutions (1 Peter 1:6–7; 4:12) and they need to stand together, no matter who is the greatest!

Commitment and character are the essentials if we are to glorify Him and have peace with each other.

The three lessons Jesus taught in this section are basic to Christian living today. If we are yielded to Him, then suffering will lead to glory, faith will produce power, and our sacrificial service will lead to honor. In spite of his impetuousness and occasional mistakes, Peter got the message and wrote: "But the God of all grace, who hath called us unto his eternal glory by Christ Jesus, after that ye have suffered a while, make you perfect, stablish, strengthen, settle you. To him be glory and dominion for ever and ever" (1 Peter 5:10–11).

QUESTIONS FOR PERSONAL REFLECTION
OR GROUP DISCUSSION

1. If you had been allowed to sit in on one of Jesus' private sessions with His disciples, what questions would you ask Him?

2. Why do you think many people failed to understand that Jesus was God's Son, even when they witnessed His miracles?

3. If you had been among the disciples when Jesus told them of His impending death, what kinds of thoughts would have run through your mind?

4. What was the relationship in Jesus' life between "suffering" and "glory"?

5. Wiersbe says that Jesus knew the crowds were following Him just because of His miracles. What better motivation for following Him did He want them to have? Why would that have been better?

6. What is the cost of being a disciple of Jesus?

7. Describe a mountaintop experience you have had that made you feel, like Peter, as if you just wanted to stay in that place and never leave.

8. Read Mark 9:24 and describe a time when you came to God with a need as this father came to Jesus. What was the result of your petition?

9. Jesus used a child to teach a lesson on humility. Why do we so often try to avoid being as humble and vulnerable as a child? What can help us change in that regard?

Chapter Eight

THE SERVANT'S PARADOXES

(Mark 10)

As a master Teacher, our Lord used many different approaches in sharing God's Word: symbols, miracles, types, parables, proverbs, and paradoxes. A paradox is a statement that seems to contradict itself and yet expresses a valid truth or principle. "When I am weak, then am I strong" is a paradox (2 Cor. 12:10; also see 2 Cor. 6:8–10). There are times when the best way to state a truth is by means of paradox, and this chapter describes our Lord doing just that. He could have preached long sermons, but instead, He gave us these five important lessons that can be expressed in five succinct, paradoxical statements.

1. TWO SHALL BE ONE (10:1–12)

Jesus completed His ministry in Galilee, left Capernaum, and came to the Trans-Jordan area, still on His way to the city of Jerusalem (Mark 10:32). This district was ruled by Herod Antipas, which may explain why the Pharisees tried to trap Him by asking a question about divorce. After all, John the Baptist had been slain because he preached against Herod's adulterous marriage (Mark 6:14–29).

But there was more than politics involved in their trick question, because divorce was a very controversial subject among the Jewish rabbis. No matter what answer Jesus gave, He would be sure to displease somebody, and this might give opportunity to arrest Him. The verbs indicate that the Pharisees "kept asking him," as though they hoped to provoke Him to say something incriminating.

In that day there were two conflicting views on divorce, and which view you espoused depended on how you interpreted the phrase "some uncleanness" in Deuteronomy 24:1–4. The followers of Rabbi Hillel were quite lenient in their interpretation and permitted a man to divorce his wife for any reason, even the burning of his food. But the school of Rabbi Shimmai was much more strict and taught that the critical words "some uncleanness" referred only to premarital sin. If a newly married husband discovered that his wife was not a virgin, then he could put her away.

As He usually did, Jesus ignored the current debates and focused attention on the Word of God, in this case, the law of Moses in Deuteronomy 24:1–4. As you study this passage, it is important to note two facts. First, it was *the man* who divorced the wife, not the wife who divorced the husband, for women did not have this right in Israel. (Roman women did have the right of divorce.) Second, the official "bill of divorcement" was given to the wife to declare her status and to assure any prospective husband that she was indeed free to remarry. Apart from the giving of this document, the only other requirement was that the woman not return to her first husband if her second husband divorced her. Among the Jews, the question was not, "May a divorced woman marry again?" because remarriage was permitted and even expected. The big question was, "What are the legal grounds for a man to divorce his wife?"

The law of Moses did not give adultery as grounds for divorce, for, in Israel, the adulterer and adulteress were stoned to death (Deut. 22:22;

Lev. 20:10; also see John 8:1–11). Whatever Moses meant by "some uncleanness" in Deuteronomy 24:1, it could not have been adultery.

Jesus explained that Moses gave the divorce law because of the sinfulness of the human heart. The law protected the wife by restraining the husband from impulsively divorcing her and abusing her like an unwanted piece of furniture, instead of treating her like a human being. Without a bill of divorcement, a woman could easily become a social outcast and be treated like a harlot. No man would want to marry her, and she would be left defenseless and destitute.

By giving this commandment to Israel, God was not putting His approval on divorce or even encouraging it. Rather, He was seeking to restrain it and make it more difficult for men to dismiss their wives. He put sufficient regulations around divorce so that the wives would not become victims of their husbands' whims.

The Lord then took them back beyond Moses to the record of the original creation (Gen. 1:27; 2:21–25). After all, in the beginning, it was *God* who established marriage, and He has the right to make the rules. According to Scripture, marriage is between a man and a woman, not two men or two women, and the relationship is sacred and permanent. It is the most intimate union in the human race, for the two become one flesh. This is not true of a father and son or a mother and daughter, but it is true of a man and wife.

While the spiritual element is vitally important in marriage, the emphasis here is that marriage is a *physical* union: the two become one *flesh*, not one spirit. Since marriage is a physical union, only a physical cause can break it—either death (Rom. 7:1–3) or fornication (Matt. 5:32; 19:9). Mark did not include the "exception clause" found in Matthew, but neither did he say that death breaks the marriage union.

Privately, the Lord further explained the matter to His questioning disciples, who by now were convinced that it was a dangerous thing to get married. To remarry after divorce, *other than one granted on the grounds of fornication,* would make the person guilty of committing adultery, and this is a serious thing. Note that Jesus included the women in His warning, which certainly elevated their status in society and gave them equality of responsibility with the men. The rabbis would not have gone this far.

Mark 10:9 warns us that *man* cannot separate those who have been united in marriage, *but God can.* Since He established marriage, He has the right to lay down the rules. A divorce may be legal according to our laws and yet not be right in the eyes of God. He expects married people to practice commitment to each other (Mark 10:7) and to remain true to each other. Too many people view divorce as "an easy way out," and do not take seriously their vows of commitment to each other and to the Lord.

2. ADULTS SHALL BE AS CHILDREN (10:13–16)

First marriage, then children; the sequence is logical. Unlike many "moderns" today, the Jews of that day looked on children as a blessing and not a burden, a rich treasure from God and not a liability (Ps. 127—128). To be without children brought a couple both sorrow and disgrace.

It was customary for parents to bring their children to the rabbis for a blessing, and so it was reasonable that they would bring the little ones to Jesus. Some were infants in arms (Luke 18:15), while others were young children able to walk, and He welcomed them all.

Why would the disciples rebuke the people and try to keep the children away from Jesus? (See Matt. 15:23 and Mark 6:36 for other instances of the disciples' seeming hardness of heart.) They probably thought they were doing Him a favor by helping Him protect His time and conserve His strength. In other words, *they did not consider the children to be important!* Their attitude was strange, because Jesus had already taught them to receive the children in His name and to be careful not to cause any of them to stumble (Mark 9:36ff.). Once again, they forgot what He had taught them.

The phrase "much displeased" is too tame. Our Lord actually became indignant as He openly rebuked His disciples for standing in the way. Then He announced that the children were better kingdom examples than were the adults. We tell the children to behave like adults, but Jesus tells the adults to model themselves after the children!

In what ways are children a pattern? In their humble dependence on others, their receptivity, their acceptance of themselves and their position in life. Of course, Jesus was speaking about an unspoiled child, not one who was trying to act like an adult. A child enjoys much but can explain very little. Children live by faith. By faith they accept their lot, trusting others to care for them and see them through.

We enter God's kingdom by faith, like little children: helpless, unable to save ourselves, totally dependent on the mercy and grace of God. We enjoy God's kingdom by faith, believing that the Father loves us and will care for our daily needs. What does a child do when he or she has a hurt or a problem? Take it to Father and Mother! What an example for us to follow in our relationship with our heavenly Father! Yes, God wants us to be childlike, but not childish!

There is no suggestion here that Jesus baptized these children, for Jesus did not even baptize adults (John 4:1–2). If the disciples had been accustomed to baptizing infants, they certainly would not have turned the people away. Jesus took these precious little ones in His loving arms and blessed them—and what a blessing that must have been!

3. The First Shall Be Last (10:17–31)

Of all the people who ever came to the feet of Jesus, this man is the only one who went away worse than he came. And yet he had so much in his favor! He was a young man (Matt. 19:22) with great potential. He was respected by others, for he held some ruling office, perhaps in a local court (Luke 18:18). Certainly he had manners and morals, and there was enough desire in his heart for spiritual things that he ran up to Jesus and bowed at His feet. In every way, he was an ideal young man, and when Jesus beheld him, He loved him.

With all of his fine qualities, the young man was very superficial in his views of spiritual things. He certainly had a shallow view of salvation, for he thought that he could *do something* to earn or merit eternal life. This was a common belief in that day among the Jews (John 6:28), and it is very common today. Most unsaved people think that God will one day add up their good works and their bad works, and if their good works exceed their bad works, they will get into heaven.

Behind this good-works approach to salvation is a superficial view of sin, man, the Bible, Jesus Christ, and salvation. Sin is rebellion against the holy God. It is not simply an action; it is an inward attitude that exalts man and defies God. Did this young man actually think that he could do a few religious works and settle his account with the holy God?

The young man had a superficial view of Jesus Christ. He called Him "Good Master" (Teacher), but we get the impression that he was trying to flatter the Lord, for the Jewish rabbis did not allow the word *good* to be applied to them. Only God was good, and the word must be reserved for Him alone. Jesus was not denying that He was God; rather, He was affirming it. He just wanted to be sure that the young man really knew what he was saying and that he was willing to accept the responsibilities involved.

This explains why Jesus pointed the young man to the law of Moses: He wanted him to see himself as a sinner bowed before the holy God. We cannot be saved from sin by keeping the law (Gal. 2:16–21; Eph. 2:8–10). The law is a mirror that shows us how dirty we are, but the mirror cannot wash us. One purpose of the law is to bring the sinner to Christ (Gal. 3:24), which is what it did in this man's case. The law can bring the sinner to Christ, but the law cannot make the sinner like Christ. Only grace can do that.

The young ruler did not see himself as a condemned sinner before God. He had a superficial view of the law of God, for he measured obedience only by external actions and not by inward attitudes. As far as his actions were concerned, he was blameless (see Phil. 3:6), but his inward attitudes were not blameless, because he was covetous. He may have kept some of the commandments, but the last commandment caught him: "Thou shalt not covet!" Covetousness is a terrible sin; it is subtle and difficult to detect, and yet it can cause a person to break all the other commandments. "For the love of money is a root of all sorts of evil" (1 Tim. 6:10 NASB). Looking at this young man, you would conclude that he had everything, but Jesus said that one thing was lacking: *a living faith in God.* Money was his god: He trusted it, worshipped it, and got his fulfillment from it. His morality and good manners only concealed a covetous heart.

Our Lord's directions in Mark 10:21 are not to be applied to everyone who wants to become a disciple, because Jesus was addressing the specific needs of the rich young ruler. The man was rich, so Jesus told him to liquidate his estate and give the money to the poor. The man was a ruler, so Jesus told him to take up a cross and follow Him, which would be a humbling experience. Jesus offered this man the gift of eternal life, but he turned it down. It is difficult to receive a gift when your fist is clenched around money and the things money can buy. The Greek word translated "grieved" gives the picture of storm clouds gathering. The man walked out of the sunshine and into a storm! He wanted to get salvation on his terms, and he was disappointed.

The disciples were shocked at the Lord's declaration about wealth, because most Jews thought that the possession of great wealth was the evidence of God's special blessing. Many people today still cling to this error, in spite of the message of Job, the example of Christ and the apostles, and the clear teaching of the New Testament. In the case of this young man, his wealth *robbed him* of God's greatest blessing, eternal life.

Today, wealth continues to make rich people poor and the first last (see 1 Cor. 1:26–31).

Money is a marvelous servant but a terrible master. If you possess money, be grateful and use it for God's glory; but if money possesses you, beware! It is good to have the things that money can buy, provided you don't lose the things that money cannot buy. The deceitfulness of riches had so choked the soil of this young man's heart that he was unable to receive the good seed of the Word and be saved (Matt. 13:22). What a bitter harvest he would reap one day!

However, Peter's response indicated that there were a few problems in his own heart. "What then will there be for us?" (Matt. 19:27 NASB). This statement reveals a rather commercial view of the Christian life: "We have given up everything for the Lord; now, what will we get in return?" Contrast Peter's words with those of the three Hebrew men in Daniel 3:16–18, and with Peter's later testimony in Acts 3:6. He certainly came a long way from "What will I get?" to "What I have, I will give!"

Jesus assured His disciples that no one who follows Him will ever lose what is really important, either in this life or in the life to come. God will reward each one. However, we must be sure our motives are right: "For my sake and the gospel's" (see Mark 8:35). The well-known Christian industrialist of the twentieth century, R. G. LeTourneau, used to say, "If you give because it pays, it won't pay!" If we sacrifice only to get a reward, that reward will never come.

Note that Jesus also promised "persecutions." He had already told His disciples what both the Jews and Gentiles would do to Him in Jerusalem, and now He informed them that they would have their share of persecution. God balances blessings with battles, developing mature sons and daughters.

To the general public, the rich ruler stood first and the poor disciples stood last. But God saw things from the perspective of eternity—and the first became last while the last became first! Those who are first in their own eyes will be last in God's eyes, but those who are last in their own eyes will be rewarded as first! What an encouragement for true disciples!

4. SERVANTS SHALL BE RULERS (10:32–45)

The destination was still Jerusalem, and Jesus was still leading the way. As Mark wrote his account of the Savior's journey to Calvary, he must have meditated much on the great "Servant Songs" in Isaiah 42—53. "For the Lord GOD will help me; therefore shall I not be confounded: therefore have I set my face like a flint, and I know that I shall not be ashamed" (Isa. 50:7). We cannot but admire the courage of God's Servant as He made His way to Calvary, and we should adore Him all the more because He did it for us.

We must try to understand the bewilderment and fear of His followers, for this was a difficult experience for them and not at all what they had planned or expected. Each new announcement of His death only added to their perplexity. In the first two announcements (Mark 8:31; 9:31), Jesus had told them *what* would occur, but now He told them *where* His passion will take place—in the Holy City of Jerusalem! In this third announcement, He also included the part that the Gentiles would play in His trial and death, and for the fourth time, He promised that He would rise again (note Mark 9:9). He told His disciples the truth, but they were in no condition to understand it.

In the light of our Lord's announcement of His death, we are embarrassed and ashamed to read of James and John asking for thrones. How could they and their mother (Matt. 20:20–21) be so callous and selfish? Peter had responded to the first announcement by arguing with Jesus; after the second announcement, the disciples responded by arguing among themselves over who was the greatest (Mark 9:30–34). These men seemed blind to the meaning of the cross.

Actually, Salome and her two sons were claiming the promise Jesus had given that, in the future kingdom, the disciples would sit on twelve thrones with the Lord Jesus. (See Matt. 19:28. Since Mark was writing especially for the Gentiles, he did not include this promise.) It took a great deal of faith on their part to claim the promise, especially since Jesus had just reminded them of His impending death. The three of them were in agreement (Matt. 18:19), and they had His Word to encourage them, so there was no reason why Jesus should not grant their request.

Except for one thing: They were praying selfishly, and God does not answer selfish prayers (James 4:2–3). If He does, it is only that He might discipline us and teach us how to pray in His will (Ps. 106:15; 1 John 5:14–15). James, John, and Salome did not realize that *it costs something to get answers to prayer.* For Jesus to grant their request, He would have to suffer and die. Why should He pay such a great price just so they could enjoy free thrones? Is that the way to glorify God?

Jesus compared His approaching suffering and death to the drinking of a cup (Mark 14:32–36) and the experiencing of a baptism (Luke 12:50; also see Ps. 41:7; 69:2, 15). It would be a devastating experience—and yet James and John said they were able to go through it with Jesus! Little did they realize what they were saying, for in later years they would indeed have their share of the baptism and the cup. James would be the first of the disciples to be martyred (Acts 12:1–2), and John would experience great persecution.

Because their prayer was motivated by earthly wisdom, not heavenly wisdom, James and John aroused the anger of the other disciples and brought disunity to the group (see James 3:13—4:1). No doubt the men were unhappy because they had not thought of asking first! Once again, Jesus tried to teach them what it means to be an "important person" in the kingdom of God (see Mark 9:33–37).

Like many people today, the disciples were making the mistake of following the wrong examples. Instead of modeling themselves after Jesus, they were admiring the glory and authority of the Roman rulers, men who loved position and authority. While there is nothing wrong with aspiring to greatness, we must be careful how we define "greatness" and why we want to achieve it. Jesus said, "Whoever wishes to become great among you shall be your servant; and whoever wishes to be first among you shall be slave of all" (Mark 10:43–44 NASB).

God's pattern in Scripture is that a person must first be a servant before God promotes him or her to be a ruler. This was true of Joseph, Moses, Joshua, David, Timothy, and even our Lord Himself (Phil. 2:1–11). Unless we know how to obey orders, we do not have the right to give orders. Before a person exercises authority, he or she must know what it means to be under authority. If Jesus Christ followed this pattern in accomplishing the great work of redemption, then surely there is no other pattern for us to follow.

5. THE POOR BECOME RICH (10:46–52)

A large crowd of Passover pilgrims followed Jesus and His disciples to Jericho, about eighteen miles from Jerusalem. There were actually two cities named Jericho: the old city in ruins, and the new city a mile away, where Herod the Great and his successors built a lavish winter palace. This may help explain the seeming contradiction between Mark 10:46 and Luke 18:35.

There were two blind beggars sitting by the road (Matt. 20:30), one of whom was named Bartimaeus. Both Mark and Luke focused attention on him since he was the more vocal of the two. The beggars heard that Jesus of Nazareth, the Healer, was passing by; they did their best to get His attention so that they might receive His merciful help and be healed.

At first, the crowd tried to silence them, but when Jesus stopped and called for the men, the crowd encouraged them! Desperate people do not permit the crowd to keep them from Jesus (see Mark 5:25–34). Bartimaeus threw off his garment so it would not trip him, and he hastened to the Master. No doubt some of the pilgrims or disciples helped him.

"What do you want Me to do for you?" seems like a strange question to ask a blind man. (It was the same question He had asked James, John, and Salome, Mark 10:36.) But Jesus wanted to give the man opportunity to express himself and give evidence of his own faith. What did he really believe Jesus *could* do for him?

When Bartimaeus called Jesus "Lord," he used the title *Rabboni,* meaning "my Master." The only other person in the Gospels who used it was Mary (John 20:16). The beggar had twice called him "Son of David," a national messianic title, but "Rabboni" was an expression of personal faith.

Matthew tells us that Jesus was moved with compassion and touched their eyes (Matt. 20:34), and immediately they were healed. Out of gratitude to Jesus, the men joined the pilgrim band and started toward Jerusalem, following Jesus. This is the last healing miracle recorded in Mark, and it certainly fits into Mark's "Servant" theme. We see Jesus Christ, God's Suffering Servant, on His way to the cross, and yet He stops to serve two blind beggars! What love, what mercy, and what grace!

QUESTIONS FOR PERSONAL REFLECTION
OR GROUP DISCUSSION

1. How would you describe our current society's view of divorce?

2. How did Jesus' mention of the wife in His directive on divorce elevate the status of women in that society? *p. 118*

3. What have the children in your life taught you about following God?

   Marriage & divorce - not to be takes lightly.

4. In Jesus' day, not to have children was a shame and a curse, and to have them was a blessing. How does that compare with our view of children today?

5. Wiersbe says that the young ruler from Mark 10 "measured obedience only by external actions and not by inward attitudes." Give some examples of measuring obedience by inward attitudes.

6. What is the most important lesson you've learned about money and its priority in your life?

7. In hindsight, it seems implausible that, in the face of Christ's servant leadership, the disciples could squabble over who would be the most important. From what you know of human nature, though, how do you imagine it happened?

8. Why does a person with a servant heart make the best leader?

9. If Jesus asked you the question that He asked Bartimaeus, "What do you want Me to do for you?" what would you answer?

Chapter Nine

THE SERVANT IN JERUSALEM

(Mark 11:1—12:44)

Jerusalem at Passover season was the delight of the Jews and the despair of the Romans. Thousands of devout Jews from all over the world arrived in the Holy City, their hearts filled with excitement and nationalistic fervor. The population of Jerusalem more than tripled during the feast, making it necessary for the Roman military units to be on special alert. They lived with the possibility that some enthusiastic Jewish zealot might try to kill a Roman official or incite a riot, and there was always potential for disputes among the various Jewish religious groups.

Into this situation came God's Servant with less than a week remaining before He would be crucified outside the city walls. In this section, we see God's Servant ministering in three different official roles.

1. THE SERVANT-KING (11:1–11)

On the road Jesus took, a traveler would arrive first at Bethany and then come to Bethphage, about two miles from Jerusalem. The elevation at this point is about 2,600 feet, and from it you have a breathtaking view of the Holy City. The Lord was about to do something He had never done before, something He had repeatedly cautioned others not to do for

Him: He was going to permit His followers to give a public demonstration in His honor.

Jesus sent two of His disciples to Bethphage to get the colt that He needed for the event. Most people today think of a donkey as nothing but a humble beast of burden, but in that day, it was looked on as an animal fit for a king to use (1 Kings 1:33). Our Lord needed this beast so that He might fulfill the messianic prophecy found in Zechariah 9:9. Mark does not quote this verse or refer to it because he was writing primarily for Gentile readers.

In fulfilling this prophecy, Jesus accomplished two purposes: (1) He declared Himself to be Israel's King and Messiah; and (2) He deliberately challenged the religious leaders. This set in motion the official plot that led to His arrest, trial, and crucifixion. The Jewish leaders had decided not to arrest Him during the feast, but God had determined otherwise. The Lamb of God must die at Passover.

Many patriotic Jews from the crowd of pilgrims eagerly joined the procession that proclaimed Jesus as the King, the Son of David come in the name of the Lord. The visitors from Galilee were most prominent in the procession, along with the people who had witnessed the raising of Lazarus from the dead (John 12:12–18). You sometimes hear it said that the same people who cried "Hosanna!" on Palm Sunday ended up crying "Crucify Him!" on Good Friday, but this is not true. The crowd that wanted Him crucified came predominantly from Judea and Jerusalem, whereas the Galilean Jews were sympathetic with Jesus and His ministry.

When welcoming a king, it was customary for people to lay their outer garments on the road, and then add festal branches (2 Kings 9:13). The shout "Hosanna!" means "Save now!" and comes from Psalm 118:25–26. Of course, Jesus knew that the people were quoting from a messianic psalm (relate Ps. 118:22–23 with Matt. 21:42–44 and Acts 4:11), but He allowed them to go right ahead and shout. He was openly affirming His kingship as the Son of David.

What were the Romans thinking as they watched this festive demonstration? After all, the Romans were experts at parades and official public events. We call this event "the Triumphal Entry," but no Roman would have used that term. An official "Roman Triumph" was indeed something to behold! When a Roman general came back to Rome after a complete conquest of an enemy, he was welcomed home with an elaborate official parade. In the parade he would exhibit his trophies of war and the illustrious prisoners he had captured. The victorious general rode in a golden chariot, priests burned incense in his honor, and the people shouted his name and praised him. The procession ended at the arena, where the people were entertained by watching the captives fight with the wild beasts. That was a "Roman Triumph."

Our Lord's "Triumphal Entry" was nothing like that, but it was a triumph just the same. He was God's anointed King and Savior, but His conquest would be spiritual and not military. A Roman general had to kill at least five thousand enemy soldiers to merit a Triumph, but in a few weeks, the gospel would "conquer" some five thousand Jews and transform their lives (Acts 4:4). Christ's "triumph" would be the victory of love over hatred, truth over error, and life over death.

After looking into the temple area, where He would return the next day, Jesus left the city and spent the night in Bethany, where it was safer and quieter. No doubt He spent time in prayer with His disciples, seeking to prepare them for the difficult week that lay ahead.

2. THE SERVANT-JUDGE (11:12–26)

Our Lord's condemning of the tree and cleansing of the temple were both symbolic acts that illustrated the sad spiritual condition of the nation of Israel. In spite of its many privileges and opportunities, Israel was outwardly fruitless (the tree) and inwardly corrupt (the temple). It was unusual for Jesus to act in judgment (John 3:17), yet there comes a time when this is the only thing God can do (John 12:35–41).

Cursing the fig tree (vv. 12–14, 20–26). The fig tree produces leaves in March or April and then starts to bear fruit in June, with another crop in August and possibly a third crop in December. The presence of leaves could mean the presence of fruit, even though that fruit was "left over" from the previous season. It is significant that in this instance Jesus did not have special knowledge to guide Him; He had to go to the tree and examine things for Himself.

If He had power to kill the tree, why didn't He use that power to restore the tree and make it produce fruit? Apart from the drowning of the pigs (Mark 5:13), this is the only instance of our Lord using His miraculous power to destroy something in nature. He did it because He wanted to teach us two important lessons.

First, there is a lesson on *failure:* Israel had failed to be fruitful for God. In the Old Testament, the fig tree is associated with the nation of Israel (Jer. 8:13; Hos. 9:10; Nah. 3:12). Like the fig tree our Lord cursed, Israel had "nothing but leaves." Note that the tree dried up "from the roots" (Mark 11:20). Three years before, John the Baptist had put the ax to the roots of the tree (Matt. 3:10), but the religious leaders would not heed his message. Whenever an individual or a group "dries up" spiritually, it is usually from the roots.

The disciples would probably connect this miracle with the parable that Jesus gave some months before (Luke 13:1–9), and they would see in the miracle a vivid picture of God's judgment on Israel. They might also recall Micah 7:1–6, where the prophet declares that God is seeking "the first ripe fruit" from His people. Christ is still seeking fruit from His people, and for us to be fruitless is sin (John 15:16). We must carefully cultivate our spiritual roots and not settle for "leaves."

Jesus also used this miracle to teach us a lesson on *faith*. The next morning, when the disciples noticed the dead tree, Jesus said, "Have faith in God," meaning, "Constantly be trusting God; live in an attitude of dependence on Him." In Jewish imagery, a mountain signifies something strong and immovable, a problem that stands in the way (Zech. 4:7). We can move these mountains only by trusting God.

Of course, this is not the only lesson Jesus ever gave on prayer, and we must be careful not to isolate it from the rest of Scripture. Prayer must be in the will of God (1 John 5:14–15), and the one praying must be abiding in the love of God (John 15:7–14). Prayer is not an emergency measure that we turn to when we have a problem. Real prayer is a part of our constant communion with God and worship of God.

Nor should we interpret Mark 11:24 to mean, "If you pray hard enough and *really believe*, God is obligated to answer your prayers, no matter what you ask." That kind of faith is not faith in God; rather, it is nothing but faith in faith, or faith in feelings. True faith in God is based on His Word (John 15:7; Rom. 10:17), and His Word reveals His will to us. It has well been said that the purpose of prayer is not to get man's will done in heaven, but to get God's will done on earth.

True prayer involves forgiveness as well as faith. I must be in fellowship with both my Father in heaven and my brethren on earth if God is to answer my prayers (see Matt. 5:21–26; 6:14–15; 18:15–35). The first word in the Lord's Prayer is *our*—"*Our* Father which art in heaven" and not "My Father which art in heaven." Though Christians may pray in private, no Christian ever prays alone, for all of God's people are part of a worldwide family that unites to seek God's blessing (Eph. 3:14–15). Prayer draws us together.

We do not earn God's blessing by forgiving one another. Our forgiving spirit is one evidence that our hearts are right with God and that we want to obey His will, and this makes it possible for the Father to hear us and to answer prayer (Ps. 66:18). Faith works by love (Gal. 5:6). If I have faith in God, I will also have love for my brother.

Cleansing the temple (vv. 15–19). Jesus had cleansed the temple during His first Passover visit (John 2:13–22), but the results had been temporary. It was not long before the religious leaders permitted the money changers and the merchants to return. The priests received their share of the profits, and, after all, these services were a convenience to the Jews who traveled to Jerusalem to worship. Suppose a foreign Jew carried his own sacrifice with him and then discovered that it was rejected because of some blemish? The money rates were always changing, so the men who exchanged foreign currency were doing the visitors a favor, even though the merchants were making a generous profit. It was easy for them to rationalize the whole enterprise.

This "religious market" was set up in the court of the Gentiles, the one place where the Jews should have been busy doing serious missionary work. If a Gentile visited the temple and saw what the Jews were doing *in the name of the true God,* he would never want to believe what they taught. The Jews might not have permitted idols of wood and stone in their temple, but there were idols there just the same. The court of the Gentiles should have been a place for praying, but it was instead a place for preying and paying.

Mark especially mentioned the people who sold doves. The dove was one of the few sacrifices that the poor people could afford (Lev. 14:22). It was the sacrifice Joseph and Mary brought when they dedicated Jesus in the temple (Luke 2:24). Even the poor people were victimized by the merchants in the temple, and this in itself must have grieved the Lord Jesus, for He was always sensitive to the poor (see Mark 12:41–44).

Jesus quoted two Scriptures to defend what He did—Isaiah 56:7 and Jeremiah 7:11. At the same time, He exposed the sins of the religious leaders. The Jews looked on the temple primarily as a place of sacrifice, but Jesus saw it as a place of prayer. True prayer is in itself a sacrifice to God (Ps. 141:1–2).

Jesus had a spiritual view of the Jewish religion, while the leaders promoted a traditional view that was cluttered with rules and regulations.

Campbell Morgan points out that "a den of thieves" is the place to which thieves run *when they want to hide*. The chief priests and scribes were using the temple and its religious services to "cover up" their sin and hypocrisy. Both Isaiah (Isa. 1:10–17) and Jeremiah (Jer. 7:1–16) had warned the people of their day that the presence of the physical temple was no guarantee of blessing from God. It was what the people did in the temple *of their hearts* that was really important. The nation had not heeded the warning of the prophets, nor would they heed our Lord's warning.

When the scribes and chief priests heard the report of our Lord's activities, they kept seeking some way to arrest Him (see Mark 14:1–2). Judas would solve the problem for them. Before we quickly condemn the Jewish religious leaders for their sins, we should examine our own ministries to see if perhaps we are making merchandise of the gospel. Do the outsiders in our community think of our church buildings as houses of prayer? Are all nations welcomed there? Do we as church members flee to church on Sundays in an attempt to cover up our sins? Do we "go to church" in order to maintain our reputation or to worship and glorify God? If the Lord Jesus were to show up in our house of worship, what changes would He make?

3. THE SERVANT-PROPHET (11:27—12:44)

In the days that followed, the representatives of the religious and political establishment descended on Jesus as He ministered in the temple, trying their best to trip Him up with their questions. He answered four questions, and then He asked them a question that silenced them for good.

A question of authority (11:27—12:12). As the official guardians of the law, the members of the Sanhedrin had both the right and the responsibility to investigate anyone who claimed to be sent by God, and that included Jesus (see Deut. 18:15–22). However, these men did not have open minds or sincere motives. They were not seeking truth; they were looking for evidence to use to destroy Him (Mark 11:18). Jesus knew what they were doing, so He countered their question with another question and exposed their hypocrisy.

Why take them all the way back to John the Baptist? For a very good reason: God does not teach us new truth if we have rejected the truth He has already revealed. This basic principle is expressed in John 7:17: "If anyone is willing to do His will, he will know of the teaching, whether it is of God or whether I speak from Myself" (NASB). "Obedience is the organ of spiritual knowledge," said the British preacher F. W. Robertson. The Jewish religious leaders had not accepted what John had taught, so why should God say anything more to them? Had they obeyed John's message, they would have gladly submitted to Christ's authority, for John came to present the Messiah to the nation.

The Jewish leaders were caught in a dilemma of their own making. They were not asking "What is true?" or "What is right?" but "What is safe?" This is always the approach of the hypocrite and the crowd-pleaser. It certainly was not the approach of either Jesus (Mark 12:14) or John the Baptist (Matt. 11:7–10). Jesus did not refuse to answer their question; He only refused to accept and endorse their hypocrisy. He was not being evasive; He was being honest.

Before they had opportunity to escape, He told them a parable that revealed *where their sins were leading them.* They had already permitted John the Baptist to be killed, but soon they would ask for the crucifixion of God's Son!

The vineyard was a familiar image of Israel (Ps. 80:8–16; Isa. 5:1–7). According to Leviticus 19:23–25, a farmer would not use the fruit until the fifth year, though we are not sure the Jews were obeying this regulation at that time. In order to retain his legal rights to the property, the owner had to receive produce from the tenants, even if it was only some of the vegetables that grew between the rows of trees or vines. This explains why the tenants refused to give him anything: They wanted to claim the vineyard for themselves. It also explains why the owner continued to send agents to them; it was purely a question of authority and ownership.

If Mark 12:2–5 covers the three years when the fruit was not used, then it was in the fourth year that the beloved Son was sent. *This is the year when the fruit was devoted to the Lord* (Lev. 19:24), and it makes the sending of the Son even more meaningful. If the tenants could do away with the heir, they would have a clear claim to the property, so they cast him out (see Heb. 13:12–13) and killed him. They wanted to preserve their own position and were willing even to kill to accomplish their evil purpose (John 11:47–53).

Jesus then asked, "What shall, therefore, the lord of the vineyard do?" The leaders answered the question first and thereby condemned themselves (Matt. 21:41), and then Jesus repeated their answer as a solemn verdict from the Judge. But before they could appeal the case, He quoted what they knew was a messianic prophecy, Psalm 118:22–23. We met this same psalm at His Triumphal Entry (Mark 11:9–10). "The Stone" was a well-known symbol for the Messiah (Ex. 17:6; Dan. 2:34; Zech. 4:7; Rom. 9:32–33; 1 Cor. 10:4; 1 Peter 2:6–8). The Servant-Judge announced a double verdict: They had not only rejected the Son, but they had also refused the Stone! There could be only one consequence—judgment (Matt. 22:1–14).

A question of responsibility (12:13–17). A common threat forced two enemies to unite, the Pharisees and the Herodians. The Herodians supported the family of Herod as well as the Romans who gave them the authority to rule. The Pharisees, however, considered the Herod clan to be the evil usurpers of the throne of David, for, after all, Herod was an Edomite and not a

Jew. The Pharisees also opposed the poll tax that the Romans had inflicted on Judea, and they resented the very presence of Rome in their land.

Their temporary alliance was a subtle trap, for no matter how Jesus replied to their question, He was in trouble with either Rome or Herod! But Jesus moved the discussion from politics to principle and caught the hypocrites in their own trap. We might state our Lord's reply something like this: "Caesar's image is on his coins, so they must be minted by his authority. The fact that you possess these coins and use them indicates that you think they are worth something. Therefore, you are already accepting Caesar's authority, or you would not use his money! But don't forget that you were created in the image of God and therefore must live under God's authority as well."

I once carried on a brief correspondence with a man who objected to my interpretation of Romans 13. He said that all government was of the Devil and that Christians must not bow to the authority of "the powers that be." I pointed out to him that even his use of the United States mail service was an acceptance of governmental authority. The money he spent buying the paper and stamps also came from the "powers that be." For that matter, the very freedom he had to express himself was a right guaranteed by—the government!

The word translated "render" in Mark 12:17 means "to pay a debt, to pay back." Jesus looked on taxes as the citizens' debt to the government in return for the services performed. Today those services would include, among other things, fire and police protection, national defense, the salaries of the officials who manage the affairs of state, special programs for the poor and underprivileged, etc. The individual Christian citizen might not agree with the way all of his tax money is used, and he can express himself with his voice and his vote, but he must accept the fact that God has established human government for our good (Rom. 13; 1 Tim. 2:1–6; 1 Peter 2:13–17). Even if we cannot respect the people in office, we must respect the office.

A question about eternity (12:18–27). This is the only place in Mark where the Sadducees are mentioned. This group accepted only the law of Moses as their religious authority; so, if a doctrine could not be defended from the first five books of the Old Testament, they would not accept it. They did not believe in the existence of the soul, life after death, resurrection, final judgment, angels, or demons (see Acts 23:8). Most of the Sadducees were priests and were wealthy. They considered themselves the "religious aristocrats" of Judaism and tended to look down on everybody else.

They brought a hypothetical question to Jesus, based on the law of marriage given in Deuteronomy 25:7–10. This woman had a series of seven husbands during her lifetime, all brothers, and all of whom had died. "If there is such a thing as a future resurrection," they argued, "then she must spend eternity with seven husbands!" It seemed a perfect argument, as most arguments are that are based on hypothetical situations.

The Sadducees thought that they were smart, but Jesus soon revealed their ignorance of two things: the power of God and the truth of Scripture. Resurrection is not the restoration of life as we know it; it is the entrance into a new life that is different. The same God who created the angels and gave them their nature is able to give us the new bodies we will need for new life in heaven (1 Cor. 15:38ff.). Jesus did not say that we would become angels or be like the angels in everything, for God's children are higher than the angels (John 17:22–24; 1 John 3:1–2). He said that in our resurrection bodies, we would be sexless like the angels, and therefore marriage would no longer exist. In the eternal state, where our new bodies are perfect and there is no death, there will be no need for marriage, procreation, and the continuance of the race.

The Sadducees were also ignorant of the Scriptures. They claimed to accept the authority of Moses, but they failed to notice that Moses taught the continuation of life after death. Once again, our Lord went back to Scripture (note Mark 2:25; 10:19; 12:10), in this case to the passage about the burning bush (Ex. 3). God did not tell Moses that He *was* (past tense) the God of Abraham, Isaac, and Jacob. He said, "I am the God of Abraham, and the God of Isaac, and the God of Jacob." The patriarchs were *alive* when God spoke those words to Moses; therefore, Moses does teach that there is life after death.

A question of priority (12:28–34). The next challenger was a scribe who was also a Pharisee (see Matt. 22:34–35). The scribes had determined that the Jews were obligated to obey 613 precepts in the law, 365 negative precepts and 248 positive. One of their favorite exercises was discussing which of these divine commandments was the greatest.

The Lord quoted Deuteronomy 6:4–5, the great confession of faith that even today pious Jews recite each morning and evening. It is called the "Shema" from the first word of the confession which means "hear." Then He quoted Leviticus 19:18, which emphasizes love for one's neighbor. Jesus made love the most important thing in life, because "love is the fulfilling of the law" (Rom. 13:8–10). If we love God, we will experience His love within and will express that love to others. We do not live by rules but by relationships, a loving relationship to God that enables us to have a loving relationship with others.

When he started this conversation, the scribe was only the tool of the Pharisees who were trying to get evidence against Jesus (note Matt. 22:35). But after he heard our Lord's answer, the scribe stood and dared to commend the Lord for His reply. The Word had spoken to the man's heart, and he was beginning to get a deeper spiritual understanding of the faith he thought he understood. Even the Old Testament Scriptures taught that there was more to the Jewish religion than offering sacrifices and keeping laws (see 1 Sam. 15:22; Ps. 51:16–17; 141:1–2; Jer. 7:22–23; Hos. 6:6; Mic. 6:6–8).

What does it mean when a person is "not far from the kingdom of

God"? It means he or she is facing truth honestly and is not interested in defending a "party line" or even personal prejudices. It means the person is testing his or her faith by what the Word of God says and not by what some religious group demands. People close to the kingdom have the courage to stand up for what is true even if they lose some friends and make some new enemies.

A question of identity (12:35–37). Now it was our Lord's turn to ask the questions, and He focused on the most important question of all: Who is the Messiah? "What think ye of Christ? Whose Son is he?" (Matt. 22:42). This is a far more important question than the ones His enemies had asked Him, for if we are wrong about Jesus Christ, we are wrong about salvation. This means we end up condemning our own souls (John 3:16–21; 8:24; 1 John 2:18–23).

Jesus quoted Psalm 110:1 and asked them to explain how David's son could also be David's Lord. The Jews believed that the Messiah would be David's son (John 7:41–42), but the only way David's son could also be David's Lord would be if Messiah were *God come in human flesh.* The answer, of course, is our Lord's miraculous conception and virgin birth (Isa. 7:14; Matt. 1:18–25; Luke 1:26–38).

This section closes with two warnings from the Lord: a warning against the pride of the scribes (Mark 12:38–40) and against the pride of the rich (Mark 12:41–44). If a person is "important" only because of the uniform he wears, the title he bears, or the office he holds, then his "importance" is artificial. It is *character* that makes a person valuable, and nobody can give you character; you must develop it yourself as you walk with God.

There were thirteen trumpet-shaped chests around the walls of the court of the women, and here the people dropped in their offerings. The rich made a big production out of their giving (see Matt. 6:1–4), but Jesus rejected them and their gifts. It is not the *portion* but the *proportion* that is important: The rich gave out of their abundance, but the poor widow gave

144 \ Be Diligent

all that she had. For the rich, their gifts were a small contribution, but for the widow, her gift was true consecration of her whole life.

Pride of living and pride of giving are sins we must avoid at all cost. How tragic that the leaders depended on a religious system that shortly would pass off the scene. How wonderful that the common people gladly listened to Jesus and obeyed His Word.

In which group are you?

QUESTIONS FOR PERSONAL REFLECTION OR GROUP DISCUSSION

1. Jesus' message and presence conflicted with both the religious and political leaders of His day. In what ways is that still true today?

   Jesus' conquest would be spiritual, not political

2. The people who welcomed Jesus at the "Triumphal Entry" into Jerusalem didn't fully understand what Jesus had come to do. What were they celebrating?

   Jesus was declaring Himself Israel's King & Messiah

3. In what ways was the Israel of Jesus' day "fruitless"?

   They were not dependent on God, not in constant communion thru prayer.

4. What did the miraculous death of the fig tree teach the disciples about God's desire for Israel?

   We must carefully cultivate our spiritual roots

5. Jesus was outraged that the temple was being used for commerce rather than prayer and worship. Does that same thing happen in our culture today? How?

6. Wiersbe asks, "If the Lord Jesus were to show up in our house of worship, what changes would He make?" What do you think?

7. Read aloud the parable in Mark 12:1–9. If the son represented Jesus and the tenants represented the religious leaders, what was the inheritance they hoped to steal from Him?

   Jesus' authority?

8. List some ways it is difficult to submit to government authorities, even though the Bible teaches they are ordained by God.

   Paying taxes

9. After reading Mark 12:18–27, how do you envision what our lives will be like when we have new life in resurrected bodies?

   Sexless bodies like the angels. Marriage would not exist

10. What does the story of the poverty-stricken widow say to you about the way you treat the money God has entrusted to you?

    By the widow giving all, she was giving more than the rich

Chapter Ten

THE SERVANT UNVEILS THE FUTURE

(Mark 13)

The Jews were proud of their temple, in spite of the fact that it was built by the Herod family in order to placate the Jews. Jesus had already given His estimate of the temple (Mark 11:15–17), but His disciples were fascinated by the magnificence of the structure. Imagine how shocked they were when Jesus informed them that the building they admired so much would one day be demolished. The Jewish leaders had defiled it; Jesus would depart from it and leave it desolate (Matt. 23:38); the Romans would destroy it.

Once away from the crowds, Jesus' disciples asked Him when this momentous event would take place and what would happen to indicate it was soon to occur. Their questions revealed that their understanding of prophecy was still quite confused. They thought that the destruction of the temple coincided with the end of the age and the return of their Lord (Matt. 24:3). But their questions gave Jesus the opportunity to deliver a prophetic message that is generally called "The Olivet Discourse" (Matt. 24—25; Luke 21:5–36).

As we study this important sermon, we must follow some practical guidelines. To begin with, we must study this discourse in the light of the rest of Scripture, especially the book of Daniel. The prophetic Scriptures harmonize if we consider all that God has revealed.

Second, we must see the practical application of the discourse. Jesus did not preach this sermon to satisfy the curiosity of His disciples, or even to straighten out their confused thinking. At least four times He said, "Take heed!" (Mark 13:5, 9, 23, 33), and He closed the address with the admonition, "Watch!" While studying this address can help us better understand future events, we must not make the mistake of setting dates (Mark 13:32)!

Third, as we study, we must keep in mind the "Jewish atmosphere" of the discourse. The Olivet Discourse grew out of some questions asked of a Jewish rabbi by four Jewish men, about the future of the Jewish temple. The warnings about "false Christs" would especially concern Jews (Mark 13:5–6, 21–22), as would the warning about Jewish courts and trials (Mark 13:9). The Jews would especially appreciate the reference to "Daniel the prophet" and the admonition to flee from Judea (Mark 13:14).

Finally, we must remember that this chapter describes a period of time known as "the tribulation" (Mark 13:19, 24; also see Matt. 24:21, 29). The Old Testament prophets wrote about this period and called it "the time of Jacob's trouble" (Jer. 30:7), a time of wrath (Zeph. 1:15–18), and a time of indignation and punishment (Isa. 26:20–21). As we shall see, it is Daniel the prophet who gives us the "key," resulting in a better understanding of the sequence of events.

In Mark 13, Jesus described three stages in this tribulation period: (1) the beginning (Mark 13:5–13); (2) the middle (Mark 13:14–18); and (3) the events that lead to the end (Mark 13:19–27). He then closed with two parables that urge believers to watch and take heed (Mark 13:28–37). Matthew's gospel is more detailed but has the same basic outline: the beginning of sorrows (Matt. 24:4–14); the middle of the tribulation (Matt. 24:15–28); the end (Matt. 24:29–31); and a closing parabolic application (Matt. 24:32–44).

I must point out that it is the conviction of many students of prophecy that believers in this present age of the church will be raptured by Christ and taken to heaven *before the tribulation begins* (1 Thess. 4:13—5:11; Rev. 3:10–11). At the close of the tribulation, they will return to earth with Christ and reign with Him (Rev. 19:11—20:6). I agree with this interpretation, but I do not make it a test of orthodoxy or spirituality.

THE FIRST HALF OF THE TRIBULATION (13:5–13)

The key statement is at the end of Mark 13:8: "These are the beginnings of sorrows." The word translated "sorrows" means "birth pangs," suggesting that the world at that time will be like a woman in travail (see Isa. 13:6–8; Jer. 4:31; 6:24; 13:21; 22:20–23; 1 Thess. 5:3). The birth pangs will come suddenly, build up gradually, and lead to a time of terrible sorrow and tribulation for the whole world.

"Don't be deceived." Jesus listed the things that must *not* be taken as the "signs" of His coming. Rather, they are indications that the tribulation "birth pangs" are just beginning. These signs are the success of false Christs (Mark 13:5–6), nations in conflict (Mark 13:7–8a), natural disturbances (Mark 13:8b), and religious persecutions (Mark 13:9–13). They have always been with us, but since these events are compared to "birth pangs," our Lord may be saying that *an acceleration of these things* would be significant.

False messiahs. The pages of history are filled with the tragic stories of false messiahs, false prophets, and their enthusiastic but deluded disciples. Jesus warned about false prophets (Matt. 7:15–20), as did Paul (Acts 20:28–31) and John (1 John 4:1–6). There is something in human nature that loves a lie and refuses to believe the costly lessons of the past. Mark Twain said that a lie runs around the world while Truth is putting on her shoes! How easy it is for spiritually blind people to follow popular leaders and gullibly accept their simple but erroneous solutions for the problems of life. Jesus warned His disciples not to be deceived by these imposters, and that warning holds good today.

Political conflicts. He also warned them not to be disturbed by political conflicts among the nations. The Roman Empire had enjoyed a measure of peace for many years, but it would not last. As the empire decayed and nationalism developed, it was inevitable that nations would come into conflict. The "Pax Romana" would be gone forever.

Natural disasters. War often leaves famine in its wake (2 Kings 25:2–3; Ezek. 6:11). Famine is also caused by man's abuse of the environment, or it can be sent by God as a judgment (1 Kings 17:1). There have always been earthquakes, and some are evidences of God's wrath (Rev. 6:12; 8:5; 11:13; 16:18). Since natural disasters have many causes, it is dangerous to dogmatically make them "the signs of the times."

"Don't be discouraged!" Not only were the believers to take heed and avoid the deceivers, but they were also to *take heed to themselves* (Mark 13:9–13). Why? Because they would face increasing opposition and persecution from sources both official (Mark 13:9–11) and personal (Mark 13:12–13). It was important that the believers use these experiences as opportunities to witness for Jesus Christ. Persecution would begin in the local Jewish courts, but it would move to the higher courts where governors and kings would be involved. You see a similar development recorded in the book of Acts (Acts 4—5; 7; 12; 16; 21—28).

But persecution would only result in proclamation! The believers would suffer *for His sake* and in that way declare His gospel. "We multiply whenever we are mown down by you," said Tertullian to his persecutors. "The blood of Christians is seed!" While I do not think that taking the gospel to all nations (Mark 13:10) is a *condition* for our Lord's return, it is certainly Christ's commission to His people (Matt. 28:19–20). The "end" here means "the end of the age," the tribulation period.

It would not be easy for these "common people" to face courts, governors, and kings, but Jesus assured them that the Holy Spirit would minister through them whenever they had opportunity to witness (Mark 13:11). This passage should not be used as an excuse or a crutch for poorly prepared preachers. It is an encouragement for all believers who sincerely want to witness for Christ and honor Him (John 14:26; Acts 4:8). If we are walking in the Spirit, we will have no trouble bearing witness for Christ when the opportunities arrive (John 15:26–27).

We can understand official persecution, but why would friends and family members create problems for believers (see Mic. 7:4ff.; John 15:18–27)? You would think that Jewish families in particular would be loyal to each other. But the Christian faith was looked on as heresy and blasphemy by both the Jews and the Gentiles. Twice daily, orthodox Jews affirmed, "Hear, O Israel: The LORD our God is one LORD" (Deut. 6:4). The Jew who said, "Jesus is Lord!" blasphemed and was worthy of death. Rome expected its citizens to declare "Caesar is lord!" or suffer the consequences. Thus, families and friends would be torn between their loyalty to their "ancient faith" and their nation, and their devotion to loved ones.

The real cause for persecution is stated in Mark 13:13: "for my name's sake." If we identify with Jesus Christ, we can expect the world to treat us the way it treated Him (John 15:20ff.). You can belong to all sorts of weird religious groups today and not suffer much opposition from family and friends, but the minute you bring the name of Jesus into the picture, and share the gospel, somebody will start to oppose you. His name is still hated.

Do not interpret Mark 13:13 as a condition for salvation, for it applies primarily to witnesses during the tribulation. In any period a person lives, if he is truly born again God will love him (John 13:1; Rom. 8:35–38) and keep him (John 10:27–29; Rom. 8:29–34). Since "the end" in Mark 13:7

means "the end of the age," that is likely what it means in Mark 13:13. During the tribulation, the true believers will prove their faith by their faithfulness. They will not give in to the godless pressures of false religion (Rev. 13).

THE MIDDLE OF THE TRIBULATION (13:14–18)

The phrase "abomination of desolation" comes from the book of Daniel and refers to the idolatrous pollution of the Jewish temple by the Gentiles. To the Jews, all idolatry is an abomination (Deut. 29:17; 2 Kings 16:3). The Jewish temple was defiled in 167 BC by the Syrian king Antiochus IV (also called "Epiphanes," meaning "illustrious") when he poured swine's blood on the altar. This event was predicted in Daniel 11:31. The temple was also defiled by the Romans in AD 70 when they captured and destroyed the city of Jerusalem. However, these events were but anticipations of the final "abomination of desolation" prophesied in Daniel 9:27 and 12:11.

In order to understand Daniel 9:24–27, we must remember that the Jewish calendar is built on a series of sevens. The seventh day of the week is the Sabbath, and the seventh week after Passover brings Pentecost. The seventh month brings the Feast of Trumpets, the day of Atonement, and the Feast of Booths. The seventh year is a sabbatical year, and after seven sabbatical years comes the Year of Jubilee.

Daniel saw seventy weeks, or periods of seven years, divinely determined for the Jews and for their Holy City, Jerusalem. This period of 490 years began with the decree of Artaxerxes in 445 BC, permitting the Jews to return to their land and rebuild Jerusalem (Ezra 1:1–4). Why must the city be restored? Because 483 years later (7 x 69), the Messiah would come to the city and give His life for sinners.

Now we must do some simple calculating. Most historians agree that Jesus was born in 5 BC, for Herod the Great was still living at the time, and he died in March, 4 BC. If our Lord died at about the age of 33, that would take us to AD 27 or 28, and this would be 483 years after 445 BC when the decree was given!

We have accounted for 483 of Daniel's 490 years, but what about the remaining 7 years? Daniel 9:27 assigns them to the tribulation period that we are now studying. (Note that Dan. 9:26 also predicts the destruction of Jerusalem—by the Romans, commentators conclude—but these two events must not be confused.) "The time of Jacob's trouble" will last seven years.

But what signals the beginning of this awful seven-year period? The signing of a covenant between the nation of Israel and "the prince that shall come" (Dan. 9:26). This "prince" is the coming world dictator that we usually call "the Antichrist." In the book of Revelation, he is called "the Beast" (Rev. 13—14). He will agree to protect Israel from her many enemies for seven years, and will even allow the Jews to rebuild their temple and restore their ancient liturgy and sacrifices. The Jews rejected their true Messiah but will accept a false messiah (John 5:43). However, after three and a half years, Antichrist will break this covenant, invade the temple, set up his own image, and force the world to worship Satan (see 2 Thess. 2:1–12; Rev. 13). This is Daniel's "abomination of desolation," and it will usher in the last half of the tribulation period, a time known as "the Great tribulation" (Matt. 24:21). Note in Mark 13:14 that Mark's parenthesis is for *readers* at a future time, not *hearers* when Jesus gave this message. This message will have special meaning to them as they see these events taking place.

Jesus gave a special warning to the Jewish believers in Jerusalem and Judea: "Get out as fast as you can!" This same warning applied when Rome attacked Jerusalem in AD 70. (See Luke 21:20–24, and remember that Daniel 9:26 predicted the invasion.) What happened in AD 70 foreshadowed what will happen in the middle of the tribulation. Dr. Harry Rimmer used to say, "Coming events cast their shadows before.

Straight ahead lies yesterday!" The warnings in Mark 13:14–18 do not apply to believers today, but they do remind us that God's people in every age must know the prophetic Word and be prepared to obey God at any time.

THE LAST HALF OF THE TRIBULATION (13:19–27)

In the book of Revelation, the last half of the tribulation is called "the wrath of God" (Rev. 14:10, 19; 15:1, 7; 16:1, 19; 19:15). During this time, God will judge the world and prepare Israel for the coming of her Messiah. It will be a time of intensive judgment such as the world has never seen or will ever see again. In it, God will be working out His purposes and setting the stage for the coming of the Conqueror (Rev. 19:11ff.).

Even in the midst of His wrath, God remembers mercy (Hab. 3:2), and for the sake of His elect, He shortens the days of the tribulation. (The "elect" refers to Israel and the Gentiles who believe during the tribulation. See Rev. 14.) To "shorten the days" means that He limits them to the three and a half years already determined and stops on time.

Satanic deception will continue to the very end, and false Christs and false prophets will lead people astray. In fact, they will even do miracles (Matt. 7:21–23; 2 Thess. 2:9–12; Rev. 13:13–14). So deceptive will be these miracles that even the elect will be tempted to believe their lies. Of themselves, miracles are not a proof of divine calling and approval (Deut. 13:1–5). The final test is the Word of God.

The tribulation period will climax with the appearing of terrifying signs in the heavens and worldwide chaos on the earth (Luke 21:25–26). These signs, which have been predicted by the prophets (Isa. 13:10; 34:4; Joel 2:10; 3:15), will prepare the way for the coming of Jesus Christ to the earth. It will be a revelation of His great glory (see Dan. 7:13–14; Mark 8:38) as He comes to establish His rule on the earth (Acts 1:11; Rev. 1:7).

Mark 13:27 describes the regathering of Israel from the nations to which they have been scattered throughout the world (Deut. 30:3–6; Isa. 11:12; Jer. 31:7–9). They will see their Messiah and trust Him, and the nation will be created in holiness and glory (Zech. 12:9—13:1; 14:4–11). That there is a glorious future for Israel is stated by Paul in Romans 11.

Jesus did not want His disciples to get so involved in the prophecies of the future that they would neglect the responsibilities of the present, so He closed the Olivet Discourse with two parables. (Matt. 25 adds three other parables—the bridesmaids, the talents, and the sheep and goats.) Note that the first parable (Mark 13:28–31) emphasizes knowing that His coming is near, while the second parable emphasizes *not knowing* the time of His return. Is this a contradiction? No, because they were addressed to two different groups of people—the first, to the tribulation saints, and the second, to all believers of every age.

The fig tree has a special association with the nation of Israel (see Mark 11:12–14, but note that Luke 21:29 adds "and all the trees"). Most of the trees in Palestine are evergreens and do not change dramatically with the seasons. Not so the fig tree; it is one of the latest to leaf out in spring, so its shoots are an indication that summer is indeed near.

As Christian believers today, we are not looking for "signs" of His coming; we are looking for Him! But people living during the tribulation will be able to watch these things occur and will know that His coming is near. This assurance will help them to endure (Mark 13:13) and to be good witnesses.

We think of a "generation" as a body of people living at the same time in history. But to what "generation" was Jesus referring in Mark 13:30? Not the generation then living in Judea, because they did not see "all these things" actually take place. Perhaps He meant the generation living during the tribulation period. But since the tribulation covers only seven years,

why refer to an entire generation? For that matter, several different generations live together during every period of history.

The Greek word translated "generation" can also mean "race, stock,
family." On several occasions, Jesus used it to refer to the Jewish nation
(Mark 8:12, 38; 9:19), and that is probably how He used it in Mark 13:30.
The chosen nation, God's elect, would be preserved to the very end, and
God would fulfill His promises to them. His Word will never fail (Josh.
21:45; 1 Kings 8:56; Matt. 24:35). We as believers do not depend on
signs; we depend on His unchanging Word, the "sure word of prophecy"
(2 Peter 1:19–21).

The parable of the fig tree cautions tribulation saints to watch and to
know the "signs of the times." But the parable of the householder warns
all of us today (Mark 13:37) to be alert, because we do not know when He
will return to take us to heaven (1 Cor. 15:51–52). Like the householder in
the story, before our Lord went from us back to heaven, He gave each of us
work to do. He expects us to be faithful while He is gone and to be working when He returns. "Take heed, watch and pray" is His admonition.

To "watch" means to be alert, to stay at one's best, to stay awake. (The
English name "Gregory" comes from this Greek word translated "watch.")
Why must we stay alert? Because nobody knows when Jesus Christ will
return. When He was on earth in His humiliation, Jesus did not know
the day or hour of His coming again. Even the angels do not know. The
unsaved world scoffs at us because we continue to cling to this "blessed
hope," but He will return as He promised (2 Peter 3). Our task is to be
faithful and to be busy, not to speculate or debate about the hidden details
of prophecy.

Watchfulness has nothing to do with going to heaven. It is purely a
matter of pleasing Him, hearing His loving commendation, and receiving
His reward (Matt. 25:14–30). There is no suggestion here that, when He
returns, Jesus will take only the faithful to heaven and leave the others on

earth to suffer the tribulation. His family is one, and He is now preparing a home for all of them, even the least worthy (John 14:1–6). We go to heaven because of His grace, not because of our faithfulness or good works (Eph. 2:8–10).

The Christians who read Mark's gospel eventually had to face intense persecution from Rome (1 Peter 4:12ff.), and this particular message must have brought comfort and strength to them. After all, if God is able to help His people witness during the great tribulation, the worst persecution of all, then surely He could strengthen the saints in the Roman Empire as they faced their fiery trial.

While Christians today will not experience the terrible sufferings described in this chapter, we will have our share of persecution and tribulation in this world before the Lord returns (John 16:33; Acts 14:22). But the warnings of this message in Mark 13 may be applied to our own lives: Take heed that you are not deceived (Mark 13:5, 23); take heed that you do not become discouraged and quit (Mark 13:9); take heed, watch and pray (Mark 13:33).

"And what I say unto you I say unto all, 'Watch'" (Mark 13:37).

QUESTIONS FOR PERSONAL REFLECTION
OR GROUP DISCUSSION

1. What is your opinion of when Jesus will return to earth?

2. How important do you think it is to discern the exact time He will return?

3. Who were some of the "false Messiahs" of the past century?

4. In what ways does life get discouraging sometimes as we wait for Christ's return?

5. Who have you known, or known of, who has experienced religious persecution?

6. How do you see religious persecution increasing in today's world?

7. Are there parts of the end times, as you understand prophecy, that frighten you? If there are, what are they?

8. What instructions does Jesus give in this chapter to those of us who are not immersed in terrible tribulation?

9. In our day-to-day lives, how can we remain alert and watchful to Christ's coming?

10. What are some things we won't do if we want to remain alert and watchful?

Chapter Eleven

THE SERVANT SUFFERS

(Mark 14:1—15:20)

While thousands of Passover pilgrims were preparing for the joys of the feast, Jesus was preparing for the ordeal of His trial and crucifixion. Just as He had steadfastly set His face to go to Jerusalem (Luke 9:51), so He steadfastly set His heart to do the Father's will. The Servant was "obedient unto death, even the death of the cross" (Phil. 2:8).

Follow His footsteps during the days and hours of the last week, and you will be amazed to see the responses of various people to the Lord Jesus Christ.

IN BETHANY—ADORED (14:1–11)

This event took place six days before Passover, which would put it on the Friday before the Triumphal Entry (John 12:1). By placing this story between the accounts of the plot to arrest Jesus, Mark contrasted the treachery of Judas and the leaders with the love and loyalty of Mary. The ugliness of their sins makes the beauty of her sacrifice even more meaningful.

Neither Mark nor Matthew names the woman, but John tells us that it was Mary of Bethany, the sister of Martha and Lazarus (John 11:1–2). Mary is found three times in the gospel stories, and each time, she is at the feet of Jesus (Luke 10:38–42; John 11:31–32; 12:1–8). Mary had a close fellowship with the Lord as she sat at His feet and listened to His Word. She is a good model for all of us to follow.

Mary's anointing of the Lord must not be confused with a similar event recorded in Luke 7:36–50. The unnamed woman in the house of Simon the Pharisee was a converted harlot who expressed her love to Christ because of His gracious forgiveness of her many sins. In the house of Simon the (healed) leper, Mary expressed her love to Christ because He was going to the cross to die for her. She prepared His body for burial as she anointed His head (Mark 14:3) and His feet (John 12:3). She showed her love for Jesus while He was still alive.

It was an expensive offering that she gave to the Lord. Spikenard was imported from India, and a whole jar would have cost the equivalent of a common worker's annual income. Mary gave lavishly and lovingly. She was not ashamed to show her love for Christ openly.

There were three consequences to her act of worship. First, the house was filled with the beautiful fragrance of the ointment (John 12:3; also note 2 Cor. 2:15–16). There is always a "spiritual fragrance" in the home where Jesus Christ is loved and worshipped.

Second, the disciples, led by Judas, criticized Mary for wasting her money! It sounded so pious for Judas to talk about the poor, when in reality he wanted the money for himself (John 12:4–6)! Even in the upper room, six days later, the disciples still thought Judas was concerned about helping the poor (John 13:21–30). It is interesting that the word translated "waste" in Mark 14:4 is translated "perdition" in John 17:12 *and applied to Judas!* Judas criticized Mary for "wasting money," but he wasted his entire life!

Third, Jesus commended Mary and accepted her gracious gift. He knew the heart of Judas and understood why the other disciples followed his bad example. He also knew Mary's heart and quickly defended her (Rom. 8:33–39). No matter what others may say about our worship and service, the most important thing is that we please the Lord. The fact that others misunderstand and criticize us should not keep us from showing our love to Christ. Our concern should be His approval alone.

When Mary gave her best at the feet of Jesus, she started a "wave of blessing" that has been going on ever since. She was a blessing to Jesus as she shared her love, and she was a blessing to her home as the fragrance spread. Were it not for Mary, her village, Bethany, would probably have been forgotten. The account of her deed was a blessing to the early church that heard about it and, because of the records in three of the Gospels, Mary has been a blessing to the whole world—and still is! The Lord's prediction has certainly been fulfilled.

Mary gave her best in faith and love; Judas gave his worst in unbelief and hatred. He solved the problem of how the Jewish leaders could arrest Jesus without causing a riot during the feast. He sold his Master for the price of a slave (see Ex. 21:32), the basest act of treachery in history.

IN THE UPPER ROOM—BETRAYED (14:12–26)

The Passover lamb was selected on the tenth day of the month of Nisan (our March-April), examined for blemishes, and then slain on the fourteenth day of the month (Ex. 12:3–6). The lamb had to be slain in the temple precincts and the supper eaten within the Jerusalem city limits. For the Jews, the Passover feast was the memorial of a past victory, but Jesus would institute a new supper that would be the memorial of His death.

Peter and John saw to it that the supper was prepared (Luke 22:8). It would not be difficult to locate the man carrying the jar of water because the women usually performed this task. Was this man John Mark's father? Did Jesus eat the Passover in an upper room in John Mark's home? These are fascinating speculations, but we have no evidence that can confirm them. However, we do know that John Mark's home was a center for Christian fellowship in Jerusalem (Acts 12:12).

The original Passover feast consisted of the roasted lamb, the unleavened bread, and the dish of bitter herbs (Ex. 12:8–20). The lamb reminded the Jews of the blood that was applied to the doorposts in Egypt to keep the angel of death from slaying their firstborn. The bread reminded them of their haste in leaving Egypt (Ex. 12:39), and the bitter herbs spoke of their suffering as Pharaoh's slaves. At some time in the centuries that followed, the Jews had added to the ceremony the drinking of four cups of wine diluted with water.

Since for the Jews the new day began with sundown, it would be Friday when Jesus and His disciples met in the upper room. This was His last Passover, and on that day, He would fulfill the Passover by dying on the cross as the spotless Lamb of God (John 1:29; 1 Cor. 5:7; 1 Peter 2:21–24).

Between Mark 14:17 and 18 are details of the washing of the disciples' feet and the lesson on humility (John 13:1–20). Following that lesson, Jesus became deeply troubled and announced that one of the disciples was a traitor. This announcement stunned all the disciples except Judas, who knew that Jesus was speaking about him. Until the very end, Jesus hid from the other disciples the identity of His betrayer, for He wanted to give Judas every opportunity to turn from sin. He even washed Judas's feet! Had Peter known the truth about Judas, he might have been tempted to kill him.

Some people try to defend Judas by arguing that he betrayed Jesus in order to force Him into revealing His power and setting up the Jewish kingdom. Others say that he was nothing but a servant who obediently fulfilled God's Word. Judas was neither a martyr nor a robot. He was a responsible human being who made his own decisions but, in so doing, fulfilled the Word of God. He must not be made into either a hero ("After all, somebody had to betray Jesus!") or a helpless victim of merciless predestination. Judas was lost for the same reason millions are lost today: He did not repent of his sins and believe on Jesus Christ (John 6:64–71;

13:10–11). If you have never been born again, one day you will wish you had not been born at all.

None of the other disciples really thought himself to be the traitor, for their questions imply a negative answer: "It is not I, is it?" The men had often debated over which of them was the greatest, but now they were discussing which of them was the vilest. To make matters worse, Jesus said that His betrayer had even eaten bread with Him at the table! In the East, to break bread with someone means to enter into a pact of friendship and mutual trust. It would be an act of the basest treachery to break bread and then betray your host. However, even this was the fulfillment of the Word of God (Ps. 41:9).

Judas was sitting in the place of honor at our Lord's left, while John was reclining to His right (John 13:23). When Jesus gave Judas the bread dipped in the herbs, it was the gracious act of a host to a special guest. Even this did not break Judas's heart, for after Judas took the morsel, Satan possessed him. Judas left the upper room to go to make the final arrangements to arrest the Lord Jesus. But even then the disciples did not know the truth about Judas (John 13:27–30), and they would not find out the truth until they met him later in the garden of Gethsemane.

After Judas left the scene, Jesus instituted what Christians commonly call "the Lord's Supper" or "the Eucharist." (The word *Eucharist* comes from a Greek word which means "to give thanks.") Before the cup, Jesus took one of the unleavened loaves, blessed it, broke it, and told the men, "This is My body." He then took the Passover cup, blessed it, and gave it to them, saying, "This is my blood" (see 1 Cor. 11:23–26).

Bread and wine were two common items that were used at practically every meal, but Jesus gave them a wonderful new meaning. When Jesus said "This is My body" and "This is My blood," He did not transform either the bread or the wine into anything different. When the disciples ate the bread, it was still bread; when they drank the wine, it was still wine.

However, the Lord gave a new meaning to the bread and the wine, so that, from that hour, they would serve as memorials of His death.

What, then, did Jesus accomplish by His death? On the cross, Jesus fulfilled the old covenant and established a new covenant (Heb. 9—10). The old covenant was ratified with the blood of animal sacrifices, but the new covenant was ratified by the blood of God's Son. The new covenant in His blood would do what the old covenant sacrifices could not do—take away sin and cleanse the heart and conscience of the believer. We are not saved from our sins by participating in a religious ceremony, but by trusting Jesus Christ as our Savior.

Our Lord's command was, "This do in remembrance of me" (1 Cor. 11:24–25). The word translated "remembrance" means much more than "in memory of," for you can do something in memory of a dead person—yet Jesus is alive! The word carries the idea of a present participation in a past event. Because Jesus is alive, as we celebrate the Lord's Supper, by faith we have communion with Him (1 Cor. 10:16–17). This is not some "magical" experience produced by the bread and cup. It is a spiritual experience that comes through our discerning of Christ and the meaning of the Supper (1 Cor. 11:27–34).

The last thing Jesus and His disciples did in the upper room was to sing the traditional Passover hymn based on Psalms 115—118. Imagine our Lord *singing* when the cross was only a few hours away!

In the Garden—Forsaken (14:27–52)

On the way to the garden of Gethsemane ("oil press"), Jesus warned the disciples that they would all forsake Him, but He then assured them that He would meet them again in Galilee after His resurrection. He even quoted Zechariah 13:7—"Smite the shepherd, and the sheep shall be scattered"—to back up His warning. Their minds and hearts were unable to receive and retain His words, for three days later, they did not believe the reports of His resurrection! And the angel had to give them a special reminder to meet Him in Galilee (Mark 16:6–7). Had they listened to His word and believed it, they would have saved themselves a great deal of anxiety, and Peter would not have denied the Lord.

The quotation from Zechariah told the disciples what to do when the Jews arrested Jesus: *scatter!* In fact, at the very time of His arrest, Jesus said, "Let these [disciples] go their way" (John 18:8). In other words, "Men, get out of here!" I have read eloquent sermons blaming Peter for "following afar off," but they completely miss the point. He was not supposed to follow at all! Had he obeyed the Lord, he would not have attacked a man with his sword or denied the Lord three times.

Peter seemed to have a difficult time applying Jesus' commands to himself. The other men might forsake Jesus, but Peter would stand true and, if necessary, go with Him to prison and to death. Of course, the other disciples echoed Peter's boast, so he was not the only self-confident one in the group. In the end, all of them failed.

When about to experience great suffering, most people want to have someone with them, to help share the burden. Often in my pastoral ministry, I have sat with people at the hospital, waiting for the surgeon to come with a report. Being perfectly human, Jesus wanted companionship as He faced the cross, and He selected Peter, James, and John, the same men who had accompanied Him to the home of Jairus (Mark 5:37) and to the Mount of Transfiguration (Mark 9:2). These three experiences parallel Philippians 3:10: "That I may know him [Mount of Transfiguration], and the power of his resurrection [home of Jairus], and the fellowship of his sufferings [garden of Gethsemane]."

Our Lord's struggle in the Garden can be understood only in the light of what would happen to Him on the cross: He would be made sin for us (2 Cor. 5:21) and bear the curse of the law (Gal. 3:13). It was not the physical suffering that almost overwhelmed Him with "anguish and sorrow," but the contemplation of being forsaken by His Father (Mark 15:34). This was "the cup" that He would drink (John 18:11). According to Hebrews 5:7–9, He asked to be saved, not "from death" but *out of death*—that is, raised from the dead—and the Father granted His request.

Abba is an Aramaic word that means "papa" or "daddy." It reveals the intimate relationship between our Lord and His Father. While believers today would probably not use that term in public, it does belong to us because we belong to Him (Rom. 8:15; Gal. 4:6). Note that Jesus did not tell the Father what to do; He had perfect confidence in God's will. Three times He prayed about the matter, and each time He yielded to the Father's will in loving surrender.

What were the three disciples doing? Sleeping! And Peter had vowed that he would die with his Lord—yet he could not even keep watch with Him! How gently Jesus rebuked the disciples and warned them. "Watch and pray" is an admonition that is often repeated in Scripture (Neh. 4:9; Mark 13:33; Eph. 6:18; Col. 4:2). It means, "Be alert as you pray! Keep your spiritual eyes open, for the enemy is near!"

The third time our Lord returned to the sleeping men, He said, "Are you still sleeping and resting? It is enough; the hour has come" (Mark 14:41 NASB). It was the hour of His sacrifice, when He would die for the sins of the world. At that moment, Judas and the temple guards arrived to arrest Jesus, and Judas kissed Jesus repeatedly as the sign that He was the one to arrest. What hypocrisy!

The fact that Judas brought such a large group of armed men is evidence that neither he nor the religious leaders really understood Jesus. They thought that Jesus would try to escape, or that His followers would put up a fight, or that perhaps He might do a miracle. Our Lord's words in Mark 14:49 were proof that He was in control, for they could have arrested Him many times earlier, except that His hour had not yet come.

Peter did a foolish thing by attacking Malchus (John 18:10), for we do not fight spiritual battles with physical weapons (2 Cor. 10:3–5). He used the wrong weapon, at the wrong time, for the wrong purpose, with the wrong motive. Had Jesus not healed Malchus, Peter would have been arrested as well, and there might have been four crosses on Calvary.

At this point, the disciples forsook Jesus and fled, and so did an unknown young man who came into the Garden and witnessed the arrest. Was this John Mark? We do not know, but since the gospel of Mark is the only one of the four gospels that records this event, the author could well have been writing about himself. If the upper room was in the home of John Mark, then perhaps Judas led the soldiers there first. John Mark may have hastily put on an outer garment and followed the mob to the Garden. The soldiers may have even tried to arrest him, so he fled.

The disciples were scattered and the Servant was now alone, "and yet I am not alone, because the Father is with me" (John 16:32). Soon, even the Father would forsake Him!

IN THE HIGH PRIEST'S PALACE—REJECTED (14:53–72)

Both the Jewish trial and the Roman trial were in three stages. The Jewish trial was opened by Annas, the former high priest (John 18:13–24). It then moved to the full council to hear witnesses (Mark 14:53–65), and then to an early morning session for the final vote of condemnation (Mark 15:1). Jesus was then sent to Pilate (Mark 15:1–5; John 18:28–38), who sent Him to Herod (Luke 23:6–12), who returned Him to Pilate (Mark 15:6–15; John 18:39—19:6). Pilate yielded to the cry of the mob and delivered Jesus to be crucified.

By the time the soldiers arrived at the palace of the high priest, Peter and John, heedless of the Lord's repeated warnings, followed the mob and even went into the courtyard. Jesus that night had sweat "as it were great drops of blood" (Luke 22:44), but Peter was cold and sat by the enemy fire!

The two disciples could not witness the actual trial, but at least they were near enough to see the outcome (Matt. 26:58; John 18:15).

After questioning and insulting Jesus, Annas sent Jesus bound to his son-in-law Caiaphas, the high priest. The Sanhedrin was assembled and the witnesses were ready. It was necessary to have at least two witnesses before the accused could be declared guilty and worthy of death (Deut. 17:6). Many witnesses testified against Jesus, but since they did not agree, their testimony was invalid. How tragic that a group of religious leaders would encourage people to lie, and during a special holy season!

Throughout this time of false accusation, our Lord said nothing (Isa. 53:7; 1 Peter 2:23). But when the high priest put Him under oath, Jesus had to reply, and He testified clearly that He was indeed the Son of God. The title "Son of man" is messianic (Dan. 7:13), and the members of the council knew exactly what Jesus was saying: He was claiming to be God come in human flesh! This claim, of course, was blasphemy to the Jews, and they declared Him guilty and worthy of death. Since it was irregular for the Sanhedrin to vote on capital cases at night, the council met again early the next morning and gave the official sentence (Mark 15:1).

While the Lord was being mocked and abused, Peter was in the courtyard below, trying to escape detection. Had he heeded the Lord's warnings, he would have avoided walking into temptation and denying his Master three times. He is a warning to all of us, for, after all, if an apostle who walked with Christ denied his Lord, what might we do in similar circumstances? The Roman believers who read Mark's gospel no doubt learned from this account, for they would soon be entering the furnace of persecution themselves.

First, one of the high priest's servant girls spoke to Peter, and he denied knowing anything about Jesus. Then the cock crowed. Another servant girl pointed Peter out to some of the bystanders, and again Peter denied knowing Jesus. Finally, a man accused him of being one of the disciples, and some of the bystanders joined in, but Peter vehemently denied knowing Jesus, and even put himself under a curse. Then the cock crowed for the second time and the Lord's prediction was fulfilled (see Mark 14:30).

However, it was not the crowing of the cock that convicted Peter; it was the remembering of Christ's words. It is always the Word that penetrates the heart and brings about true repentance. Peter pondered what Jesus had said and what he himself had done, and then Jesus, on His way to Pilate's hall, turned and looked at Peter. It was a look of love, to be sure, but *injured* love (Luke 22:61). His heart broken, Peter went out quickly and wept bitterly.

Before we judge Peter too severely, we need to examine our own lives. How many times have we denied the Lord and lost opportunities to share the gospel with others? Do we, like Peter, talk when we should listen, argue when we should obey, sleep when we should pray, and fight when we should submit? Peter at least was sorry for his sins and wept over them, and the Lord did forgive him. After His resurrection, Jesus had a private meeting with Peter (Luke 24:34); then Jesus helped Peter make a public confession when He met the disciples in Galilee (John 21).

IN PILATE'S HALL—CONDEMNED (15:1–20)

As soon as their early morning meeting was over, and the verdict officially recorded, the Jewish leaders delivered Jesus to the Roman governor, Pontius Pilate. The governor usually resided at Caesarea, but it was his custom to be in Jerusalem each year for the feast. His presence pleased some of the Jews, and he could be on hand if any problems arose among the thousands of people crowded into Jerusalem. Roman governors held court early in the morning, so he was quite prepared when they brought the prisoner to him.

The Jewish council had to convince Pilate that Jesus was guilty of a capital crime and therefore worthy of death (John 18:31–32). In spite of their political corruption, many Roman officials had an appreciation for justice and tried to deal fairly with prisoners. Furthermore, Pilate had no great love for the Jews and was not about to do them any favors. He knew that the Jewish leaders were not interested in seeing justice done; what they really wanted was vengeance (Mark 15:10).

John gives us the most details of the Roman trial, and when you combine the gospel records, you discover that Pilate repeatedly stated that he found no fault in Jesus (John 18:38; Luke 23:14; John 19:4; Luke 23:22; Matt. 27:24). His problem was that he lacked the courage to stand for what he believed. He wanted to avoid a riot (Matt. 27:24), so he was "willing to content the people" (Mark 15:15). Pilate did not ask, "Is it right?" Instead, he asked, "Is it safe? Is it popular?"

The council had only one capital crime that they might be able to present to Pilate: Jesus claimed to be a king and He stirred up the people. They tried to pass Him off as a dangerous revolutionary who was undermining the authority of Rome. As Pilate questioned Jesus, the Lord said nothing, but the chief priests kept accusing Him and trying to wear down the governor's resistance.

Pilate thought he could avoid making a decision by sending Jesus to Herod, the ruler of Galilee (Luke 23:6–12), but Herod only sent Jesus back after mocking Him. Then the governor offered the people a choice—Jesus the Nazarene, or Barabbas, the murderer and insurrectionist—thinking that surely sanity would prevail and they would ask to have Jesus released. But the chief priests had prepared the crowd carefully (Mark 15:11), and they asked for Barabbas to be set free and Jesus to be crucified.

The governor then tried a third ruse: He had Jesus scourged, hoping that the sight of the suffering prisoner would somehow arouse their pity (Mark 15:15; John 19:1ff.). But the plan did not work. The governor gave in and delivered Jesus to be crucified.

Then followed the disgraceful mockery by the soldiers, as they beat Him, spat on Him, and bowed in mock homage. Roman soldiers would certainly laugh at a Jew who claimed to be a king! "We have no king but Caesar!" (John 19:12–15). Our Lord quietly suffered and did not fight back, a lesson that Mark's readers would need to learn as they faced official persecution (1 Peter 2:21–24).

But men had not yet done their worst to God's Son. Now they would lead Him outside the city and nail Him to a cross, and the Servant would die for the sins of the very people who were crucifying Him.

QUESTIONS FOR PERSONAL REFLECTION
OR GROUP DISCUSSION

1. How can we follow Mary's example of making Jesus a priority by taking time to be with Him and honor Him?

2. How easy is it for you to worship Jesus with the kind of passion that Mary showed?

3. If you had been a disciple at the Last Supper, what would you have thought when Jesus said His traitor was among you?

4. When Jesus prayed in the garden, the disciples slept. What do you think was their perspective on the situation that allowed them to be so casual about it?

5. What does the fact that a large group of men came to arrest Jesus tell you about their understanding (or misunderstanding) of Jesus?

6. Peter was in real danger when those in the courtyard asked him about knowing Jesus. What can cause us to feel afraid or embarrassed when someone questions us about Jesus?

7. How do we sometimes deny Christ today?

8. How do you explain the drastic change in the people's attitudes from their cheers during Jesus' entry into Jerusalem to their jeers during His trial and crucifixion?

9. The charge against Jesus was that He claimed to be king and stirred up the people. In what ways were those charges true or false?

Chapter Twelve

THE SERVANT FINISHES HIS WORK

(Mark 15:21—16:20)

Cecil Rhodes devoted his life to British expansion in South Africa, plus making a fortune in diamonds. He was not yet fifty years old when he died, and his last words were, "So little done, so much to do."

"I have glorified thee on the earth," Jesus said to His Father; "I have finished the work which thou gavest me to do" (John 17:4). It would be wonderful if all of us could give that same kind of report when we get to the end of life's journey. To know that we have accomplished His work and glorified His name would certainly make us look back with thanksgiving and ahead with excitement and anticipation.

The four events described in this final section of Mark give us the climax of the gospel story and the historical basis for the message of the gospel (1 Cor. 15:1–8).

1. THE SERVANT'S DEATH (15:21–41)

Three specific hours are mentioned in this section of Mark: the third (Mark 15:25), the sixth (Mark 15:33), and the ninth (Mark 15:33–34). The Jews reckoned time from 6:00 a.m. to 6:00 p.m., so this means that the third hour was 9:00 a.m., the sixth hour noon, and the ninth hour 3:00 p.m. Mark followed the Jewish system, whereas the apostle John used Roman time in his gospel. This means that "the sixth hour" in John 19:14 is 6:00 a.m.

The third hour (vv. 21–32). According to law, the guilty victim had to carry his cross, or at least the crossbeam, to the place of execution, and Jesus was no exception. He left Pilate's hall bearing His cross (John 19:16–17), but He could not continue, so the soldiers "drafted" Simon of Cyrene to carry the cross for Him. Roman officers had the privilege of "impressing" men for service, and the way they used this privilege irritated the Jews (Matt. 5:41).

When you consider all that our Lord had endured since His arrest, it is not surprising that His strength failed. Indeed, "He could have called ten thousand angels," yet He willingly bore the suffering on our behalf. There was a higher purpose behind this act: The victim carried the cross because he had been found guilty, *but our Lord was not guilty.* We are the guilty ones, and Simon carried that cross on our behalf. Simon Peter boasted that he would go with Jesus to prison and to death (Luke 22:33), but it was Simon of Cyrene, not Simon Peter, who came to the aid of the Master.

In one of his folksy letters to his mother, Harry Truman wrote, "I went to the White House to see the President and discovered I was the President." Simon had come to Jerusalem to celebrate the Passover (Acts 2:10; 6:9), and he ended up meeting the Passover Lamb! We have good reason to believe that Simon trusted the Savior and went home and led his two sons to the Lord. No doubt many of Mark's Roman readers knew Alexander and Rufus (Rom. 16:13), and perhaps they had even known Simon.

Golgotha is a Hebrew word that means "skull," though nowhere does the text explain why the place bore that name. Visitors to the Holy Land today are shown "Gordon's Calvary," which does have the appearance of a skull, but guides also point out another possible site in the Church of the Holy

Sepulchre. We do not know the exact place where our Lord was crucified, nor is it important that we know. He was crucified outside the city walls, the place of rejection (Heb. 13:12–13), and He died for the sins of the world.

It was customary for the victims to be given a narcotic potion that would help deaden the pain (Prov. 31:6), but our Lord refused it. For one thing, He wanted to be in full possession of His faculties as He did the Father's will and accomplished the work of redemption. He would enter fully into His sufferings on our behalf and take no shortcuts. He refused the cup of sympathy so that He might better drink the cup of iniquity (Matt. 26:36–43). What an example for us to follow as we do God's will and share "the fellowship of his sufferings" (Phil. 3:10).

None of the gospel writers gives us a description of crucifixion, nor is one necessary. Their aim is not to arouse our pity but to assure our faith. Many of their readers had probably witnessed crucifixions, so any details would have been unnecessary. Crucifixion was such a detestable thing that it was not mentioned in decent society, any more than today we would discuss the gas chamber or the electric chair. Suffice it to say, crucifixion is one of the most horrible forms of death ever devised by man. Read Psalm 22 for a description of some of our Lord's agonies as He hung on the cross.

The victim usually wore a placard that declared his offense. Pilate wrote the one that Jesus wore and that was later hung above Him on the cross: "This is Jesus of Nazareth, the King of the Jews." The Jewish leaders protested, but Pilate for once stood his ground (John 19:19–22). It may be that the message of this sign first aroused the hopes of the repentant thief (Luke 23:39–43). He may have reasoned: "If His name is Jesus, then He is a Savior. If He is from Nazareth, then He would identify with rejected people (John 1:46). If He has a kingdom, then perhaps there is room for me!"

The soldiers at the execution were not only doing their duty, but they were also fulfilling prophecy as they gambled for our Lord's garments (Ps. 22:18). The fact that the innocent Son of God was placed between two guilty criminals also fulfilled prophecy (Isa. 53:12; and see Luke 22:37). The word used for "thieves" is rendered *robber* in John 18:40 in reference to Barabbas, so perhaps these two men had been members of his rebel band.

It seems incredible that the religious leaders so hated Jesus that they even went out to Golgotha to mock Him. Thomas Carlyle called ridicule "the language of the Devil," and in this case, that definition is certainly true. The idle spectators who passed by were only too eager to follow the bad example of their leaders, so enduring mockery was added to the sufferings of our Lord. They mocked Him as Prophet (Mark 15:29), as Savior (Mark 15:31), and as King (Mark 15:32). It is possible that their sarcastic "He saved others!" may have encouraged the one thief to trust Him. The thief may have reasoned, "If He saved others, then He can save me!" So God uses even the wrath of man to praise Him (Ps. 76:10).

The sixth hour (v. 33). At noon, a miraculous darkness came over the land, and all creation sympathized with the Creator as He suffered. This was indeed a miracle and not some natural phenomenon, such as a sand storm or an eclipse. It would not be possible to have an eclipse during full moon at Passover. By means of this darkness, God was saying something to the people.

For one thing, the Jews would certainly think about the first Passover. The ninth plague in Egypt was a three-day darkness, followed by the last plague, the death of the firstborn (Ex. 10:22—11:9). The darkness at Calvary was an announcement that God's Firstborn and Beloved Son, the Lamb of God, was giving His life for the sins of the world. It was also an announcement that judgment was coming and men had better be prepared.

The ninth hour (vv. 34–41). Our Lord made seven statements from the cross, three of them before the darkness came: "Father, forgive them; for they know not what they do" (Luke 23:34); "Today shalt thou be with me in paradise" (Luke 23:43); and "Woman, behold thy son.… Behold thy mother" (John 19:26–27). When the darkness came, there was silence on His cross, for it was then that He was made sin for us (2 Cor. 5:21).

At the ninth hour, Jesus expressed the agony of His soul when He cried out from the cross, "My God, my God, why hast thou forsaken me?" (see Ps. 22:1). The darkness symbolized the judgment Jesus experienced when the Father forsook Him. As was so often the case, the people did not understand His words; they thought He was calling for Elijah the prophet. There was not only darkness over the land, but there was darkness in the minds and hearts of the people (2 Cor. 4:3–6; John 3:16–21; 12:35–41).

Then Jesus said, "I thirst" (John 19:28), and the kind act of the soldier in giving Jesus a sip of vinegar (see Ps. 69:21) assisted Him in uttering two more wonderful statements: "It is finished!" (John 19:30) and "Father, into thy hands I commend my spirit" (Luke 23:46; and see Ps. 31:5). Jesus was not murdered; He willingly laid down His life for us (John 10:11, 15, 17–18). He was not a martyr; He was a willing sacrifice for the sins of the world.

Two remarkable events occurred at His death: There was an earthquake (Matt. 27:51), and the veil in the temple was torn in two. The veil had separated man from God, but now, through His death, Jesus had opened for the whole world a "new and living way" (Heb. 10:12–22; also see John 14:6). There had been an earthquake at Sinai when the law was given (Ex. 19:16–18), but now the law was fulfilled in Jesus Christ and its curse removed (Rom. 10:4; Gal. 3:10–14). Through His sacrifice, Jesus had purchased not only freedom from the law, but also freedom from the entire sacrificial system.

It is thrilling to read the witness of the Roman centurion, especially when you consider that his words could have gotten him into trouble with both the Jews and the Romans. That Jesus Christ is the Son of God is one of Mark's important themes (Mark 1:1, 11; 3:11; 5:7; 9:7; 14:61–62). This makes His servanthood even more wonderful (Phil. 2:1–11).

It is touching to see how the women stood near the cross until the very end. John had also been there, but he had taken Mary, our Lord's mother, to his own home where he could care for her (John 19:25–27). Faithful women were the last at the cross on Friday and the first at the tomb on Sunday. What a contrast to the disciples, who had boasted that they would die for Him! The church of Jesus Christ owes much to the sacrifice and devotion of believing women.

2. THE SERVANT'S BURIAL (15:42–47)

The Jews recognized two evenings: "early evening" from three to six o'clock, and "evening" after six o'clock, when the new day would begin. This explains how both Matthew (27:57) and Mark could call late Friday afternoon "evening." It was important that the place of execution be quickly cleared, because the Jewish Sabbath was about to begin, and that Sabbath was a "high day" because of the Passover (John 19:31).

God had a wealthy member of the Sanhedrin, Joseph of Arimathea, ready to take care of the body of Jesus (Matt. 27:57). He was assisted by Nicodemus, also a member of the council (John 19:38–42). We must not think that these two men suddenly decided to bury Jesus, because what they did demanded much preparation.

To begin with, Joseph had to prepare the tomb in a garden near the place where Jesus died. This tomb was probably not for Joseph himself, since a wealthy man would not likely choose to be buried near a place of execution. The men also had to obtain a large quantity of spices (John 19:39), and this could not be done when the shops were closed for Passover. And all of this had to be done without the council's knowledge.

It seems evident that God prepared these two men and directed them in their activities. Nicodemus had come to Jesus privately (John 3) and had even defended Him before the council (John 7:45–53). I believe that Joseph and Nicodemus searched the Scriptures together and discovered, led by the Spirit, that the Lamb would die at Passover. It is possible that they were hiding in the new tomb when Jesus died. It was a simple matter for Joseph to go to Pilate for permission to take the body, and for Nicodemus to guard the body until the official release was given. Had these men not acted boldly, the body of Jesus might have been disposed of like rubbish.

It was important that His body be prepared for burial so that the empty graveclothes could be left behind in the tomb (John 20:1–10). Also, the way He was buried fulfilled prophecy (Isa. 53:9). The fact that He was buried is proof that Jesus actually died on the cross, for the Roman officials would not have released the body without proof that Jesus was dead.

3. THE SERVANT'S RESURRECTION (16:1–18)

Jesus Christ was "delivered for our offenses, and was raised again for our justification" (Rom. 4:25). A dead Savior cannot save anybody. The resurrection of Jesus Christ from the dead is as much a part of the gospel message as His sacrificial death on the cross (1 Cor. 15:1–8). In fact, in the book of Acts, the church gave witness primarily to the resurrection (Acts 1:22; 4:2, 33).

The resurrection proves that Jesus Christ is what He claimed to be, the very Son of God (Rom. 1:4). He had told His disciples that He would be raised from the dead, but they had not grasped the meaning of this truth (Mark 9:9–10, 31; 10:34). Even the women who came early to the tomb did not expect to see Him alive. In fact, they had purchased spices to complete the anointing that Joseph and Nicodemus had so hastily begun.

When you combine the accounts in the Gospels, you arrive at the following probable order of resurrection appearances on that first day of the week: (1) to Mary Magdalene (John 20:11–18 and Mark 16:9–11); (2) to the other women (Matt. 28:9–10); (3) to Peter (Luke 24:34 and 1 Cor. 15:5); (4) to the two men going to Emmaus (Mark 16:12 and Luke

24:13–32); and (5) to ten of the disciples in the upper room (Mark 16:14 and John 20:19–25).

It was still dark when Mary Magdalene, Mary the mother of James, Salome, and Joanna (Luke 24:10) started out for the tomb (John 20:1), and they arrived at early dawn (Luke 24:1). Their first surprise was finding the stone already rolled away from the door (Matt. 28:2–4) so that they were able to enter into the tomb. The second surprise was meeting two angels in the tomb (Luke 24:4; Mark focused on only one angel), and the third surprise was hearing the message they delivered. No wonder the women were amazed!

The message was that Jesus was not there: He had risen from the dead, and He was going before them into Galilee where He would meet them. The women were the first messengers of the glorious resurrection message! Note that there was a special word of encouragement for Peter (Mark 16:7), and keep in mind that Mark wrote his gospel with Peter's assistance.

Mary Magdalene ran to tell Peter and John what she had discovered (John 20:2–10), and then she lingered at the tomb after they left. It was then that Jesus appeared to her (John 20:11–18). From her conversation with Jesus, it seems that Mary did not fully grasp what the angels had said, but she was the first believer to see the risen Christ. Mark 16:8 may give the idea that all the women fled, but Mark 16:9 states that Mary met Jesus personally.

After He appeared to Mary, Jesus met the other women as they were on their way to report their conversation with Jesus to the disciples (Matt. 28:9–10). Initially, the women were both joyful and afraid, but after they met the risen Christ, they found the disciples and shared the good news (Matt. 28:8). It is one thing to hear the message and quite something else to meet the risen Lord personally. When you meet Him, you have something to share with others.

The emphasis in Mark 16:9–14 is on the unbelief of the disciples, who were mourning and weeping instead of rejoicing at the good news. Was it because they were prejudiced against the witness of the women? Perhaps, for the testimony of a woman was not accepted in a Jewish court. But even when the two Emmaus disciples gave their witness, not everybody believed. (Compare Mark 16:13 with Luke 24:33–35.) Apparently there was division in the upper room until Jesus Himself appeared.

But when He did appear, He reproached them for their unbelief, which was caused by their hardness of heart (see Mark 6:52; 8:17). He was making it clear that the witnesses of His resurrection could and should be trusted. The phrase "the eleven" in Mark 16:14 simply means "the apostles," because there were only ten of them together at that time, since Thomas was absent (John 20:19–25).

Before His ascension forty days later, the Lord gave several commissions to His followers (Matt. 28:18–20; Luke 24:47–49; John 20:21; 21:15–17; Acts 1:4–8). The one Mark gives probably is a part of the Great Commission that Jesus gave on a mountain in Galilee (Matt. 28:16–20).

In this commission, Jesus pointed out our message and our ministry, and then backed it up with the miraculous credentials that only He could give. The message is the gospel, the good news of salvation through faith in Jesus Christ. The ministry is to share this message with the whole world.

A superficial reading of Mark 16:15–16 would suggest that sinners must be baptized to be saved, but this misinterpretation disappears when you note that the emphasis is on *believing*. If a person does not believe, he is condemned, even if he has been baptized (see John 3:16–18, 36). It was expected in the early church that believers would be baptized (Acts 2:41; 10:44–48).

When God sent Moses to challenge Pharaoh in Egypt, He gave him special miracles to perform as his divine credentials, proving that he was sent from God (Ex. 4:1–9). This was also true of some of the prophets (1 Kings 18; 2 Kings 2:14–25). The apostles were also given special "signs" that enforced their message (Acts 19:11–12; 2 Cor. 12:12; Heb. 2:3–4).

186 \ Be Diligent

Of themselves, miracles do not prove that a person has been sent by God, for the message must also be true to God's Word (see 2 Thess. 2; Rev. 13).

Most of the signs listed here did take place in the days of the apostles and are recorded in the book of Acts. The closest thing we have to taking up serpents is Paul's experience on Malta (Acts 28:3–6), but we have no biblical record of anyone drinking poison and surviving. No doubt God has performed many wonders for His own that we know nothing about, but we shall learn about them in heaven.

It is tragic when well-meaning but untaught people claim these signs for themselves and then die because of snake bites or poison. Of course, the excuse is given that they did not have enough faith! But whatever is not of faith is sin (Rom. 14:23); therefore, they should not have done it in the first place.

The person who takes up serpents just to prove his or her faith is yielding to the very temptation Satan presented to Jesus on the pinnacle of the temple (Matt. 4:5–7): "Cast Yourself down and see if God will take care of You," Satan said in effect. He wants us to "show off" our faith and force God to perform unnecessary miracles. Jesus refused to tempt God, and we should follow His example. Yes, God cares for His children when, in His will, they are in dangerous places, but He is not obligated to care for us when we foolishly get out of His will. We are called to live by faith, not by chance, and to trust God, not tempt Him.

4. THE SERVANT'S ASCENSION (16:19–20)
In a remarkable way, the gospel of Mark parallels the great "Servant passage" in Philippians 2:

He came as a Servant (Phil. 2:1–7)—Mark 1—13
He died on a cross (Phil. 2:8)—Mark 14—15
He was exalted to glory (Phil. 2:9)—Mark 16

Both Paul and Mark emphasize the need for God's people to get the message out to all nations (Mark 16:15–16; Phil. 2:10–11), and there is the added assurance that God is at work in and through them (Mark 16:19–20; Phil. 2:12–13).

Our Lord's ascension marked the completion of His earthly ministry and the beginning of His new ministry in heaven as High Priest and Advocate for His people (Heb. 7—10; 1 John 2:1–3). The "right hand of God" is the place of honor and authority (Ps. 110:1; 1 Peter 3:22). Our Lord is like Melchizedek, King of Righteousness and King of Peace (Gen. 14:17–19; Heb. 7:2).

One of His heavenly ministries is that of enabling His people to do His will (Heb. 13:20–21). It is fitting that the gospel of the Servant should end with this reference to work, just as it is fitting for Matthew, the gospel of the King, to end with a reference to His great authority. By His Holy Spirit, the Lord wants to work *in* us (Phil. 2:12–13), *with* us (Mark 16:20), and *for* us (Rom. 8:28).

The apostles and prophets laid the foundation for the church (Eph. 2:20), so their work is finished and the apostolic signs have ceased. But the Lord's working has not ceased, and He is still working in and through His people to save a lost world. His Servant-Son Jesus returned to heaven, but He still has His people on earth who can be His servants, if they will.

What a privilege to have the Lord working with us!

What an opportunity and obligation we have to carry the gospel to the whole world!

"For even the Son of man came not to be ministered unto, but to minister, and to give his life a ransom for many" (Mark 10:45).

Are you serving—or are you expecting others to serve you?

QUESTIONS FOR PERSONAL REFLECTION
OR GROUP DISCUSSION

1. What would it take to face torture and death as Jesus did, when He knew He had the power to remove Himself from it?

2. What do you think convinced one of the thieves hanging on a cross beside Jesus to ask for Jesus' help?

3. Why do you suppose the religious leaders of Jesus' day hated Him so much that they stood at His execution and continued to mock Him?

4. When Jesus died, the curtain that served as a door to the holiest place in the temple was ripped open. What does that symbolize for you in terms of your access to God?

5. During the time between Jesus' death and resurrection, what kind of conversations do you think the disciples had?

6. How would you answer those who argue that Jesus didn't really die on the cross, but only passed out and woke later?

7. As Jesus spent time with His disciples between His resurrection and ascension, what memories do you think they relived together?

8. How does Jesus' resurrection affect your day-to-day life?

9. When Jesus ascended back into heaven, He left us with a mission and a responsibility. How do you live out that mission?

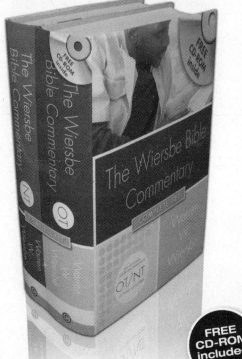